THE CAPTIVE PARTY

The Captive Party

How Labour was taken over by Capital

Michael Barratt Brown

What has happened and what could happen to the British Economy

Mr Mandelson's Friends   3

'A Party of Business'   8

What Are They up to? On Whose Agenda?   19

The Private Finance Initiative Everywhere   29

A Manufacturing or Service Economy?   40

Private Profit or Public Provision?   51

A Way Out of the Dilemmas?   61

'Public-private partnerships are all about negotiating deals that are good for both sides. The private sector wants to earn a return on its ability to invest and perform. The public sector wants contracts where incentives exist for the private sector supplier to deliver services on time to specified standards year after year. In that, the public sector shares an *absolute identity of interest* [emphasis added] with private financiers whose return on investment will depend on these services being delivered to those standards.'

– Gordon Brown, 'Foreword' *Partnerships for Prosperity: the Private Finance Initiative*, London: Treasury Task Force, 1997

'The problem we've got is that the intellectually cogent evidence we're hearing is against PFI [Private Finance Initiative], but the government and the sponsors aren't going to like it.'

– a member of the Institute for Public Policy Research's Commission on Public-Private Partnerships, as reported by Nick Cohen, 'What real influence does the centre-left and Labour's favourite think-tank wield?', *New Statesman*, 21.08.00, pp.14-15

Quotations taken from Sally Ruane, senior lecturer in Health Studies, De Montfort University, Leicester, 'A clear public mission? Public-private partnerships and the recommodification of the NHS', *Capital and Class*, issue 73, Spring 2001

'What has often been cited as an irresoluble clash in socialist theory between regulating material production according to human needs and the principle of eliminating the exploitative domination of man over man can only be met through producers controlling the organisation of the production process. Thus it is precisely the surging forward of demands by trade unionists for real control over the decisions affecting their livelihood that will be the point of departure for socialists.'

Gordon Brown, 'Introduction: The Socialist Challenge', *The Red Paper on Scotland*, edited by Gordon Brown, published in 1975 by EUSB, Edinburgh.

Chapter One

Mr Mandelson's Friends

Who was Captivating Whom?

Peter Mandelson, Tony Blair's right hand man, joint author of *The Blair Revolution* and one-time holder of three cabinet posts, first as Minister without Portfolio, then as Trade and Industry Secretary, finally as Secretary of State for Northern Ireland, called himself 'Labour's ambassador to the rich, powerful and well-connected'. Those whom he captivated with his charm included not only Mr. Srichand Hinduja of passport fame and of course Geoffrey Robinson, who lent him £373,000 for a smart house and lost them both their ministerial jobs for doing it, but, so it appeared, even royalty – Princess Margaret and Camilla Parker-Bowles. More importantly the list according to press reports included several of Britain's top business people:

Sir Evelyn Rothschild, President of Rothschild's Bank
Sir Dennis Stevenson, Chairman of Pearsons, publisher of the
  Financial Times
Gavyn Davies, merchant banker and BBC Vice-Chairman
Elizabeth Murdoch , managing director of BskyB
Robert Bourne, chairman of Legacy which is bidding for the Dome site
Lord Waheed Alli, broadcasting tycoon
Lord Birt, former BBC Director General
Jamie Palumbo, member of the Dome consortium

Murdoch, Bourne and Waheed Alli were all substantial Labour donors. This fine list was said to be complemented by important political persons with no long-standing Labour connections:

Lady Carla Powell, wife of Sir Charles Powell, personal adviser to Mrs Thatcher when Prime Minister and brother of Jonathan Powell, who is Mr Blair's *chef de cabinet* as Prime Minister
Howell James, adviser to John Major when Prime Minister
Shaun Woodard, former Tory MP now a Labour backbencher.

We know all this because *The Scotsman* of Friday January 5, 2001 carried a full-page story with coloured pictures of them all including Mr Mandelson in front of a large birthday cake. This was after *The Times* newspaper had claimed that Mr Bourne and his wife with several of those listed above celebrated Mr Mandelson's birthday in October 1999 at a lavish party which Tory MP, and shadow Cabinet Office Minister, Andrew Lansley, was complaining should have been declared in the Register of Members' interests. Mr Bourne, chairman of the Legacy consortium, was reported by *The Scotsman* to be a donor to the Labour Party as well as a bidder for the Dome site for a knock-down sum of £165 million. The Tories may just be jealous, but it does raise the question of who was captivating whom.

A very special friend of Peter Mandelson who was reported by *The Scotsman* at the birthday party was Roger Liddle, one-time Social Democrat, and now a member of the Prime Minister's kitchen cabinet, who was the joint author with Peter Mandelson of *The Blair Revolution* that launched the Blair project in 1996. Liddle was one of those whose name was mentioned in the cash for access scandal with that of Derek Draper, who was Mandelson's personal assistant at the time when Mandelson was in charge of making a success of the Dome, for which he fatally sought Mr Srichand Hinduja's support and much else. On cash for access Draper got the chop and probably would not have been invited to the birthday party, to judge by his comment (*Guardian*, 24.01.01) on the Hinduja passport affair, not only that 'There must be someone at the Home Office gunning for Peter.' But that 'He should stay away from rich, glamorous people, because he seems to go gaga every time he meets one.' Draper should know. Perhaps he was just envious after he had done so much work for Mandelson in that direction in the past.

Together with those already listed above who may have been at the birthday party, there were certainly reports in *The Scotsman* of a galaxy of 'rich and glamorous people' from the media and show business among Mandelson's friends: Jon Snow, Mick Jagger, Tom Stoppard, Jeremy Irons and Sinead Cusack, Sabrina Guinness, Anne McElvoy, Robert Harris.

The Blair Project

This story has become rather more important than it seemed at the time. Of course, it could all be dismissed as a little bit of innocuous socialising between government and business friends. The Tories always did it. You never knew with them, as Mr Justice Lynskey put it in a famous Tribunal, whether on the grouse moors the ministers and the bankers were counting the bag or deciding on a change in the bank rate. But Peter Mandelson is/was Labour, and his connections with London Society must be the closest of any leading Labour Party member since Ramsay MacDonald became the darling of the duchesses in the 1930s. And what happened to him? He left Labour to form a National Government with Liberals and Tories – the equivalent today of the dream coalition that never was of Tony Blair and Paddy Ashdown. It could still come, and Liberal Democrats like Roy Jenkins, Social Democratic Party founder and chair of the Commission on Proportional Representation, and Roger Liddle, ex-SDP member now a Tony Blair adviser, are at hand to help. Liddle is the one whom Gregory Palast embarrassingly quoted in *The Observer* explaining to an American business man how to make friends and influence people in the New Labour establishment.

If the electorate proves to be as cynical when it comes to voting as it sounds before the election, a coalition government could come next time and, with PR to follow, we could have coalitions for ever. 'Breaking the mould', the Social Democrats called it – they certainly broke the Labour Party by their defection. There wouldn't then be a Labour Party. It was different in 1931 when Ramsay MacDonald defected. There was still a Labour Party with socialist leaders of modest mien like George Lansbury and Clement Attlee to reverse the MacDonald-Lady Limerick image. In this little book we shall argue that the links between Labour and business, that is with Capital (with a capital C), have become so close that this time round we should have to create a new party of Labour and at the end of the book we will think about what that would mean.

In the next chapter we shall look at Labour's business links in detail to see what they amount to. We shall find that Peter Mandelson's charm offensive and his social parties were no more than the tip of a very large iceberg. Below our gaze, and often carefully concealed from our eyes, there is a great mass of interlocking connections between the New Labour government and big business, both British and American. George Monbiot, of the *The Guardian*, to whom I am indebted for giving me the idea for the title of this pamphlet, has described these connections as 'the corporate take-over of Britain', making Britain into a 'Captive State'. This is, thus, the title of the book in which Monbiot reveals just how far big business has already moved in to take over not only Britain's industries, but the farms, towns, roads, hospitals, schools, universities, prisons, passports and, we have to add, the foreign and defence policy of the country.

I have quoted from Monbiot's book at length, especially in chapter 2, partly because of the detailed and telling nature of his evidence, partly because of the embarrassed silence which appears to have greeted its publication – no response from New Labour, no MPs' questions and hardly any mention in the press and other media. Apart from critical reviews, in *The Times* from Howard Davies, former head of the Confederation of British Industry, in *The Independent* from David Attenborough, and in the *New Statesman* from Mick Hume, former editor of *Living Marxism*, there was nothing – not in the *FT*, *The Observer*, *Economist*, *Telegraph*, *Mail*, *Scotsman*, nothing on TV, in the regional press, just one radio spot. As John Vidal commented in reviewing Monbiot in *The Ecologist*, 'in the US it might have won a Pulitzer prize and then been made into a celebrated defamation case … in Germany or the Nordic countries there would have been an inquiry.' That is not the English way; here the truth is quietly buried. Monbiot's lectures are closely monitored, he claims (*The Guardian* 01.02.01) because he is said to be a 'security risk' and universities should not give him cover. Fortunately, there is much to be discovered on the internet by clicking on to Red Star Research – http:/www.red-star-research.org.uk – and I have made much use of this source, as also of the Unison web-site Unison.org.uk.

We shall be looking in particular at the links with United States capital and here the role of Peter Mandelson takes on something more than a social aspect. Gregory Palast in *The Ecologist* (April 2000) revealed a fascinating story of 13 business trips outside Britain made by Mandelson during the months January to September 1999, when he was out of office, but evidently not out of work. Three of these were to the United States, apparently on the private plane of Linda Wachner, American ladies undergarment tycoon, with whom he stayed it is said in August 1998, while still Secretary of State for

Industry, which is less important than his main destinations in 1999. These were the Progressive Foundation and the Aspen Institute, arms of the Democratic Leadership Conference, the directorate of Clinton's Party, and the ultra-Right Hudson Institute's Regulatory Institute. Mandelson's trip to Portugal in June 1999 had also an American connection, since it was to the Bilderberg Conference that brings bankers and politicians together.

When Ken Coates and I wrote in 1996, some months before New Labour was elected, a book in response to Mandelson and Liddle's *The Blair Revolution: Can New Labour Deliver?*, we called our book *The Blair Revelation: Deliverance for Whom?* We outlined the Blair project as it was unfurling and emphasised that at its heart was to be found a project to make labour acceptable to capital and to preserve the 'special relationship' with the United States. Everything that has happened in the last five years has confirmed our very worst expectations. For more than two years government spending was kept down to the lowest levels of Conservative governments. The yawning gaps were filled by inviting private capital in to make private profits through the Private Finance Initiative and other devices. The Tory privatisation programme was not halted, let alone turned back; it was accelerated – on the railways, the London Underground, at the airports and even with Air Traffic Control. Then, when new government money was released – for schools, hospitals, energy, roads, railways, housing, prisons – again and again it was linked to private capital and private profit, with all too often American companies to the fore. As so much else with New Labour, the United States has suggested the model. US investment houses, one of whose leading members, Gavyn Davies, was on the Mandelson list, have said that services comprise the fastest growing sector in world trade, with health, education and water shaping up to be the most profitable. So that's it.

Chapter Two
'A Party of Business'

At the 1997 General Election, New Labour, wishing not to be seen as too dependent on Trade Union funding, looked for donations from rich businessmen. These included a donation of £1 million from Bernie Ecclestone, the king of Formula One motorcar racing, but when it was discovered that concessions had been made by the government for tobacco advertising on the racing circuits, a million pound cheque was sent back. Many other large donations were not returned, for example one of £2 million from Lord Sainsbury, who became a cabinet minister under New Labour. For the General Election of 2001 New Labour has already notched up three donations of £2 million each, another one from Lord Sainsbury, one from Mr Christopher Ondaatje and one from Lord Hamlyn. Since two of these men were already peers, there can be no accusations of buying honours there.

The Labour benches in the House of Lords have, however, been strengthened recently by the addition of Lord Haskins of Northern Foods, a regular Labour donor, Lord Levy of Chase Music, Lord Paul of Caparo Industries, his company a major Labour donor (over £100,000 in 1998), Lord Alexander Bernstein, former chair of Granada, a major donor (£200,000 in 1999), Lord Bragg (Melvyn) an old LWT colleague of Mandelson and a major Labour donor (£25,000 in 1997), Lord Robert Gavron, former director of the St. Ives printing group and former Chairman of the Guardian Media Group, a major donor (£500,000 in each of 1996, 1997 and 1999), Lord Waheed Alli, managing director of Planet 24 Television, which is a Labour donor, George Simpson of GEC and Andrew Stone of Marks and Spencer. And then there are Lord Puttnam of Anglia Television and Lord Hollick of United Business Media, both long standing New Labour supporters, who both sit on the Government's Creative Industries Task Force along with two more Labour donors Alan McGee of Creation Records and Lord Waheed Alli, and Sir Richard Branson, who is not a Labour donor. Perhaps mention should be made here of other old LWT colleagues besides Lords Bragg and Bernstein, who are major Labour donors and recently elevated to high places: Gerry

Robinson, Chairman of the Granada Group and now Head of the Arts Council and Greg Dyke, new Director General of the BBC.

New Labour's Task Forces: A New Social Formation

New Labour has, we begin to see, to a remarkable degree opened up its ranks to leading businessmen, both in government and in the vast range of QUANGOs which it has created. According to an Essex University research group, Democratic Audit, 320 Task Forces with more than 2500 members have been set up since Labour took office, there being no previous Tory equivalent. A table in *The Economist* (14.08.99) showed that 28 of Britain's 100 biggest companies – the *Financial Times* Stock Exchange (FTSE) 100 – had provided either their chairman or chief executive or both as part-time advisers on such bodies, or sometimes on full-time appointments to the Government. With regard to the membership of these task forces, Democratic Audit revealed that only 2% in 1999 came from Trade Unions. On the Treasury Task Forces 96 out of 108 places were filled by business leaders (90%), and on the Department of Trade and Industry list the proportion was 75%. Many names occur more than once, like that of Peter Agar from the Confederation of British Industry, Lord Marshall formerly chair of British Airways and Sir Chris Evans, of Citygrove Leisure, a London based property development company which was a Labour donor in 1999.

What this amounts to is a new social formation of Business and New Labour. It is clear that many of those involved come from the giant transnational companies, in particular from the oil companies and those engaged in chemicals, pharmaceuticals and bio-technology, in all of which British capital has a strong world-wide presence. In looking at the individuals who have been drawn from business into the 'Blair Project', it is necessary to relate them in each case to the Task Force to which they have been assigned. These are the men and a few women whom George Monbiot has listed in the 'Fat Cats Directory' in his book *The Captive State*, and I have drawn heavily on this list in what follows, to supplement what can be found in *Red Star Research* on the internet, from which there is detailed information available on the Oil and Gas Task Forces, the Better Regulation Task Force, the Creative Industries Task Force and some others.

The leading business figure in the New Labour firmament is undoubtedly Lord Sainsbury, the Minister of Science in the Department of Trade and Industry. One-time supporter of the Liberal Democrats, Lord Sainsbury was chairman of J.Sainsbury plc and chairman of the Food Chain Group, but has become best known for his links with Diatech, the biotechnology company with important genetic engineering patents, and the Sainsbury Laboratory at the John Innes genetic engineering centre in Norwich. As Science Minister he has overall charge of the Government's Foresight Programme and he has ultimate responsibility for the Biotechnology and Biological Sciences Research Council, which helps to finance the Sainsbury Laboratory. The Government's Chief Scientific Adviser explains that 'Lord Sainsbury always leaves the room whenever GM food is discussed.' But he has on the BBC publicly defended the government's position on GM foods and he is reported to have accompanied members of the Bio-Industry Association, including Diatech, on a visit to the USA, partly funded by the UK Department of Trade and Industry.

Oil and Gas to the Fore

The Government's Oil and Gas Industry Task Force, set up by Lord (Gus) Macdonald, the new minister from the Scottish Media Group, and its successor called Task Force 2 (PILOT) are dominated by the big oil companies. We find Malcolm Brindred, chairman of Shell UK, Alan Jones succeeded by Steve Marshall, successive regional presidents of BP-Amoco Scotland, John Macdonald, managing director of Texaco North Sea Ltd., Syd Fudge, former Chief Executive of Kvaerner Oil and Gas, chair of the Offshore Contractors Association, Mark Hope, Technical Director of Enterprise Oil, and George Watkins, managing director of Conoco. Most of these companies and TotalFinaElf are represented on the Fuel Supply Task Force, which was set up by Tony Blair following the blockade of oil refineries in September 2000.

The oil companies have furthermore supplied one of their chairmen as a New Labour minister. Second only to Lord Sainsbury in New Labour's business hierarchy is Lord Simon of Highbury, formerly chairman of BP, the giant oil and gas company. Lord Simon was Minister for Trade and Competitiveness in Europe in the Department of Trade and Industry, responsible for negotiations in the European Union of a common energy tax and liberalisation of the gas market. In this role he harried British MEPs in 1997 (according to the *Sunday Telegraph* of 3.8.97) to water down the workers' rights directive in the European Union company takeover law and later, in 1998, according to the TUC General Secretary John Monks, required the blocking of such rights in the Competition and Transfer of Rights directive. Lord Simon argued in both cases that these matters were not for European Union decision under the subsidiarity principle and were more properly dealt with by self-regulation. This created a big row in 1997, when Lord Simon was accused of having a conflict of interest, since he still held £2 million worth of shares in BP, which he had not declared in the Lords register of members' interests. His explanation like that of Lord Sainsbury, when similarly accused, was that they were held in a 'blind trust' over which he had no control. The explanation was accepted.

Apart from the BP chairmanship Lord Simon was also vice-chairman of the European Round Table of Industrialists, who not only helped to draft and see through the Single European Act but also planned a still wider trans-Atlantic single market. This was to introduce American laws, standards and practices throughout the market. The French revolted and the plan was dropped, but taken up again by the so-called Trans-Atlantic Economic Partnership, itself the off-spring of the Trans-Atlantic Business Dialogue (TABD). The members of this Dialogue include such companies as Philips, ICI, Unilever, Siemens, Boeing, Ford, Procter and Gamble and Time-Warner. Its aim according to Timothy Hauser, US Under-Secretary of Commerce, is 'to identify those barriers to trade or opportunities for liberalisation on which both business communities [US and EU] could agree as targets for government action.' Lord Simon was also one of the Ministers responsible for implementing Britain's 'ethical foreign policy', but according to John Redwood, Tory shadow Trade and Industry Secretary at the time, 'Robin Cook would not have [him] at the Foreign Office.' (*Daily Telegraph*, 25.07.97)

This is not the end of BP's links with government, however. A BP director sits on the Council for Science and Technology and, until the end of 1998, Sir John Cadogan, formerly BP's Research Director, was the Director General of the UK's Research Councils. A lady (for once) Judith Hanratty, company secretary of BP-Amoco plc, the controversial merger of two of the world's biggest oil companies, appropriately sits on the board of the Government's Competition Commission. In the year 2000 BP-Amoco took over Atlantic Richfield and Burma Castrol, making it almost the largest of the world's oil companies. University posts are not of course gifts of government, but there are BP professorships, fellowships or lectureships at seven British universities including both Oxford and Cambridge. All will be hoping for grants for their researches from the UK Research Councils.

If BP was one of New Labour's leading business friends, it could hardly be that Shell would be left far behind; and sure enough, Chris Fay, the ex-chairman and chief executive of Shell UK, has a role to play in the New Labour project. Mr Fay was also an Executive Director of BAA plc which is attempting to double the size of Heathrow airport, with the help of Lord Rogers, the architect and another of Monbiot's 'fat cats' in the chair of the Government's Urban Task Force. More important for the Government, Mr Fay is the President of the UK Offshore Operators' Association, an industry lobby group which has resisted increased taxes on the oil companies' recently enlarged profits, but has also fiercely resisted attempts to introduce new environmental regulations. Quite appropriately, therefore, Mr Fay is chairman of the government's Advisory Committee on Business and the Environment. It is perhaps somewhat more surprising that Shell is responsible for running the London Borough of Lambeth's Education Action Zone.

Protecting the Environment

It must mean something that neither BP-Amoco nor Shell provide the Chair for Gordon Brown's Energy Tax Review. This is supplied by British Airways, the largest single user of energy, in the formidable shape of Lord Marshall, former British Airways' chairman. Lord Marshall was also president of the Confederation of British Industry and as such once warned Gordon Brown not to levy new taxes on corporations aimed at reducing the contribution to global warming.

The business team that mans the Environment Agency is a remarkable mixture, as we learn from George Monbiot, quoting from ENDS Reports, Friends of the Earth, and other sources. The chair of the Agency was Lord de Ramsey, who was also President of the Country Landowners' Association, which has repeatedly warned the Government against imposing 'unjustified' environmental 'burdens' on agriculture. Lord de Ramsey has apparently grown GM sugar beet on his land at Ramsey for Monsanto. The Country Landowners also have their next President, Ewan Cameron, who fought the Government's right to roam proposals, as Chairman of the Government's Countryside Commission. The Commission is responsible for implementing the right to roam.

The actual head of the Environment Agency Protection Directorate is a Mr Paul Leinster, who was a Director of Smithkline Beecham (SB) plc, which has been accused of polluting streams in Sussex and Gloucestershire. Leinster was previously employed by BP and Schering Agrochemicals, part owner of AgrEvo, which was named and shamed for failing to comply with government regulations concerning the testing of genetically engineered crops. All these gentlemen come under the direction of a lady, Ms. Dinah Nichols, who is Director General of Environmental Protection at the Department of the Environment. She was previously a non-executive director of Anglia Water, which came sixth in 1999 in the Environment Agency's 'hall of shame' after six prosecutions for pollution.

In a prestigious list of this sort we would expect to find ICI, and indeed there is ICI Katalco's Managing Director, Justin McCracken, as regional manager of the Environment Agency in the North West region. In 1999 ICI topped the list of the Environment Agency's 'hall of shame', its list of companies fined most heavily for pollution incidents in England and Wales. One of ICI's worst acts of pollution occurred actually in the North-West region in 1998, when ICI was fined £300,000 after 150 tonnes of chloroform escaped into ground water at Runcorn. Friends of the Earth recorded 244 unauthorised pollution incidents from ICI's Runcorn plant in 1996 and 1997.

Zeneca, which was once a part of ICI and deeply involved in genetically engineered crops including collaboration with the John

Innes Institute in Norwich, has two representatives on the Government's research and environmental committees. Peter Doyle, who was a Zeneca executive director is the chair of the Biotechnology and Biological Sciences Research Council; and Professor Nigel Poole, who as Zeneca's External and Regulatory Affairs Plant Science Manager, sat on five of the task forces run by EuropaBio, the GM lobbying organisation in the European Union, and is on the Government's Advisory Committee on Releases to the Environment. Zeneca had had six applications to release GM organisms approved by the Advisory Committee on Releases to the Environment. Biotechnology is also represented in government by Keith McCullough, who was Chief Executive Officer of British Biotech, a company censured by the Stock Exchange for serious rule breaches of information. Mr. McCullough is now Chair of the Government's Finance Advisory Group.

It may be that the New Labour Government is being very clever in setting a thief to catch a thief, or it may be not. Sir Anthony Cleaver, who was Executive Director of Smith & Nephew Pharmaceuticals and Chairman of Atomic Energy Technology plc, and oversaw the changes at Dounreay nuclear power station, which were heavily criticised by the Health and Safety Executive, is Chairman of the Government's Medical Research Council. Ian MacAllister, Chairman and Managing Director of Ford UK and President of the Society of Motor Manufacturers and Traders, which has lobbied against European Union directives aimed at reducing exhaust gases, is the Chairman of the Government's Cleaner Vehicles Task Force. Professor Peter Schroeder who was Director of Research and Development at Nestlé, well known for its baby food, is Director of the Government's Food Research Council. Tony Edwards, a director of the TI Group, which owned Matrix Churchill, the famous supplier of machine tools for arms manufacture to the Iraqi government, is Head of the Government's Defence Export Services Organisation, which advises the Government on arms sales to foreign governments.

Some Contradictions in Regulation
One of the Government's Task Forces is entitled the 'Better Regulation Task Force'. 'Better Regulation' is evidently a euphemism

for 'Deregulation', since its remit is to save businesses from what they see as 'unnecessary' regulation. This Task Force is chaired by Lord Haskins, chairman of Northern Foods, a Labour donor and supporter over many years. It has on it Ian Peters, deputy director of the Confederation of British Industry (CBI), who is also on Gordon Brown's European Monetary Union Advisory Group, Simon Ward, Director of Strategic Affairs at Whitbread, the brewers, Sarah Anderson, Chief Executive of the Mayday Group and chair of the CBI's Small and Medium Enterprise Council, Peter Hughes, Chief Executive of the lobbying group, Scottish Engineering, Balram Gidoomal, millionaire Chairman of Winning Communications, Ann Shaw chair of the Institute of Directors (Northern Ireland Branch), and Sue Slipman (a leading Communist Party member who resigned to help found the Social Democratic Party), now Director for Social Responsibility of the Camelot Group. Among former members of this Task Force were Sir Simon Gourlay, former President of the National Farmers' Union, Peter Salisbury ex-Chief Executive of Marks and Spencer, Anthony Tinsley of Unilever, Hugh Field of CBC International medical equipment suppliers, and Pamela Meadows, former director of the right-wing Policy Studies Institute.

There is particular interest in the presence on this Task Force of Dr Chai Patel, a Labour donor, Chief Executive Officer and Managing Director of Westminster Health Care, Britain's third largest nursing home company, because he was the Chair of the Task Force's Working Group on the Department of Health's 'action team' on NHS bed use. It recommended transferring older patients from hospitals into homes and nursing homes with appropriate financial support. This subject came up recently (see Will Hutton, *The Observer*, 28.01.01) when the Scottish Parliament rejected a Government ruling that living and hotel costs should be means tested where old people were transferred from hospitals, although a commission on long term social care had recommended universal free personal care. It will be interesting to see how the Task Forces deal with that.

The list of contradictions on the Task Forces goes on and on. Stephanie Munk, a highly paid lady, receives £230,000 with £205,000 in stock options as Human Resource Director for the Granada Group. The Group recently had a strike on their hands by workers, presumably part-time, whose pay was cut from £140 to £100 a week. Ms. Munk is a member of the Government's Low Pay Commission and New Deal Task Force. She is joined on this Task Force by Sir Peter Davis, one-time Chief Executive of Prudential Corporation plc, which was condemned by the Treasury for mass mis-selling of pensions. David Bowman, a director of Commercial Union, which was also named by the Treasury for supposedly mis-sold pensions, is on the board of the Occupational Pensions Regulatory Authority.

David Steeds is a key person in the new world of private finance initiatives. From being Corporate Development Director of Serco plc, one of the most successful bidders for privately financed government projects, he is Chief Executive of the Government's Private Finance Panel. Jonathan Rickford, director of corporate strategy at BT, which has been under criticism for the size of its market share, is on the board of the Competition Commission. Peter Salsbury, already mentioned as the ex-Managing Director for Corporate and External Affairs at troubled Marks and Spencer, was until September 2000 head of the Better Regulation Task Force's special Consumer Affairs Group, whose task includes protection of consumers from the superstores. Sir Alastair Morton, the Channel Tunnel construction consortium chairman, now combines advising John Prescott on the financing of the Channel Tunnel rail link with Chairmanship of the Government's Strategic Rail Authority. A colleague of Sir Alastair's on the Channel Tunnel, merchant banker Adrian Montague, heads the Treasury Task Force for the Private Finance Initiative.

This is not the end of Monbiot's 'Fat Cats Directory'. Construction firms are well connected with Government projects and AMEC plc seems to be in the lead. Sir Alan Cockshaw, the Chairman of AMEC plc, is now Chairman of the Government's Commission for New Towns and Chairman of the Government land development agency, English Partnerships. The Deputy Chairman of this important agency is Michael Mallinson, formerly President of the British Property Federation, the property developers' lobby group. Another AMEC director, Peter Mason, the Chief Executive Officer, sits on the Export Credit Guarantees Advisory Council. AMEC has received large credits for overseas contracts from the Export Credit Guarantee Department (ECGD). Another AMEC non-executive director, Liz Airey, also sits on the Advisory Council. AMEC has lobbied against the imposition of environmental and human rights conditions on ECGD loans. There is still another AMEC Director, Mike Straughton, Services Director, who sits on the Oil and Gas Industry Task Force 2 (PILOT)

Most astonishing is the story of Robert Osborne who was Head of the Special Projects Division of Tarmac, which is a major builder of privately financed hospitals commissioned by the Department of Health. In 1997 he became Chief Executive of the Department of Health's Private Finance Unit, an appointment that was then criticised by Chris Smith when he was shadow Health Secretary on the ground of conflict of interest. When Osborne returned to Tarmac in January 1998, with the inside knowledge gained in the Department, there was no protest from the Government, and in the year 2000 the Private Finance Unit was privatised. From hospitals to prisons, Sue Clifton, an executive at Group 4, which runs two private jails which handle children in Britain and has been the subject of serious criticism, is adviser to the Government's Youth Justice Board on the handling of juvenile offenders. Finally we have to note that Neville Bain, a non-executive director of Safeway, which has been busily swallowing local branches of the Post Office, has been appointed by the Government as Chairman of the Post Office.

One 'fat cat' not so far listed cannot be overlooked. That is Geoffrey Robinson, chair of Transfer Technology plc, a company formed by the merger of Transtec, Robinson's own company, with Central & Sherwood plc, a property company owned and chaired by Robert Maxwell of ill fame. Transtec later collapsed but left Robinson still a multi-millionaire. Blair made Robinson his Paymaster General with special responsibility for the energy industries. What he did in that post we shall see later. That is before he had to resign in the scandal over the undeclared loan of £373,000 to Peter Mandelson, at that time Secretary of State for Trade and Industry, a department which was just then examining a complaint against Robinson in relation to his previous financial interests.

At the end of this review, we have to conclude that these men, and a few women, from British business are not just advisers to Government ministers. Four, Lord Sainsbury, Lord McDonald, Lord Simon and Geoffrey Robinson, were actually brought into government as Ministers. Many on the list are Chairmen or Chief Executive Officers of what are in effect organs of government, whether these are Task Forces, Working Parties, Commissions, Action Teams, Agencies, Special Units, Authorities, Working Groups or other Special Groups. In the case of the Treasury Task Force its executive role on the Private Finance Initiative has been taken over by *Partnerships UK*, chaired by director of Prudential with a deputy from the city house of Kleinwort Benson, a business board and a large staff to promote public private partnerships by sponoring contractual agreements.

We have still to hear an authoritative statement from inside the civil service about the effect that these new organs of government have on the machinery of government and the responsibility of ministers. What we know is that the Treasury has been steadily advancing its position over the ministries, especially Social Security. After the first statement by Gordon Brown at the beginning of this book this would be in line with what we have seen. Critics like Professor Peter Townsend have warned that the Treasury under Brown is aiming for a permanent 'two-tier society', as the earlier Gordon Brown would have understood.

It is evident that when Tony Blair claimed that 'Labour was the Party of Business' he really meant it. Labour and capital had come together in a new way. But what have they been doing together? We shall have to probe further.

Chapter Three

What Are They Up To?
On Whose Agenda?

In Education and Health

No one can doubt, after reading the last chapter, that there is any question about the increasingly close links between government and business under New Labour. There remains a question about who is working for whom. It could be that New Labour has simply harnessed the expertise of Big Business to carry through its own agenda. This agenda was laid down by Tony Blair at a Labour Party Conference. A Labour Government would, he said, 'set the people free' creating 'a model 20th Century nation based on ... the equal worth of all.' This was to be in line with the new Clause Four of the Labour Party's Constitution, under which we were all to be 'stakeholders' in UK plc, following 'a new conception of community ... where all citizens have a stake and a sense of social justice and fairness govern (sic) decision-making by those in power'. It was a stake, but only 'a sense' of social justice, and some people would definitely be 'in power'. As we have noted, they spoke of Labour as 'the Party of Business' which aimed to establish 'the most business-friendly environment in the world'. It could be that Blair still believed he was following his own agenda, but that in fact business had taken over the agenda, or perhaps they had just come to have the same agenda. Gordon Brown after all says that they have 'absolute identity of interest'. We need to look closely at what has actually been happening.

We can go back to the 1999 Labour Party conference, when delegates found that they had to make their way into the hall past 62 corporate stalls advertising their goods and services. When asked by the BBC whether the exhibitors there were buying access to ministers, Lord Whitty replied, 'You don't buy access to ministers. You buy access to the whole Party.' George Monbiot recording this reply comments that perhaps 'he was trying to reassure us'. It is access to ministers that Monbiot's book reveals and what he calls 'the corruption to which our political leaders have succumbed.' Is it really as bad as that? Or is it best described as a new social formation that is emerging? Let us see.

We may begin with education – Tony Blair's 'Education, Education, Education!' When New Labour entered office, the UK came last but three (Japan, Poland and Italy) of all 25 industrial countries in a League Table of spending on education taken as a percentage of national income. In government spending alone the UK came below Poland. Although UK taxation was taking a lower proportion of UK national income than it was in other countries of the European Union, bar only Spain and Portugal, there was a serious question of where the money would come from to meet the needs of education as well as other urgent needs in the Health Service, in housing, transport and the environment. The New Labour Government was committed to keeping within the tax limits set by its Conservative predecessor, but did impose a once-for-all 'windfall tax' on the profits of the privatised utilities companies.

Universities

Business representatives in the UK had for long been complaining about the inadequacies of the products of the British education system – low levels of literacy, lack of numeracy, poor innovative capacity. The Dearing Committee on Higher Education, which reported in 1997, put great emphasis on the need for the UK to 'compete in increasingly competitive markets ... where ... our international competitors are aiming to improve the contribution higher education systems make to their economic performance'. Their vision of the 'learning society' which they looked for emerging in the UK over the next 20 years was of 'an economically successful nation' 'at the leading edge of world practice'. In stressing the importance of recruiting mature students into 'life-long learning' the Committee insisted that this should 'enable higher education to be responsive to the needs of local industry and commerce.' In a specially commissioned Committee report (no.12) the benefits for employers to be derived from the allocation of more resources to education were listed: value added from directly usable skills, screening of potential employees' abilities, bidding down of wages from increased graduate supply.

At the end of all that it might have been supposed that the

Committee would recommend an increase in the contribution to be made by employers to increased expenditure on higher education. Their contribution in 1995-6 was some 2.7% of the total costs, although this did not include some direct sponsorship of students. 2.7% of the total amounted to about £300 million, which could be compared with annual company profits of around £30,000 million in that year. The Committee, however, concluded that 'the *burden* (emphasis added) on employers of employment and training costs ... would simply add to employment costs' – and presumably thereby reduce competitiveness. They therefore recommended that students should pay – to the extent of £1000 a year – towards their fees.

The New Labour Government accepted this recommendation and in addition ended the payment of grants towards accommodation and living costs, substituting in their place a system of student loans to be paid back over time. In a 1998 White Paper the Government launched 'a reach-out fund to encourage universities to work more closely with business.' The Higher Education Funding Council was redefined, 'to ensure that higher education is responsive to the needs of business and industry.'

Paid educational leave, which alone would make the aim of life-long learning realisable, was not considered either in the Dearing Report or in the subsequent Fryer Report on Continuing Education and Life-long Learning, and this despite the abysmal lack of education in the labour force revealed by the latter. Only 40% of 18 year olds were currently in any kind of training or education, and only 14% of all employees took part in job-related training. At the same time the finance provided by Big Business for Universities was quite specifically directed to research of direct benefit to the companies concerned. The subjects of the company-sponsored professorships at Cambridge, for example, tell their own story: the Shell Chair in Chemical Engineering, BP professorships in Organic Chemistry and Petroleum Science, an ICI Chair in Applied Thermodynamics, a Glaxo Chair of Molecular Parasitology, a Unilever Chair of Molecular Science, a Price Waterhouse Chair of Financial Accounting, a Marks and Spencer Chair of Farm Animal Health and Food Science, a Montagu Burton Chair of Industrial Relations. AT&T, BP, Microsoft, Rolls Royce and Zeneca all have laboratories in the University. The oil companies alone are said to have 1000 research projects being conducted at British universities. BP, Esso and Shell are all represented on the Higher Education Funding Council which allocates Government funds to universities.

We have already noted Lord Sainsbury's important connections with university research and the position of Peter Doyle from Zeneca as Chairman of the Biotechnology and Biological Sciences Research Council. The BBSRC provides the government funding for most biologists working in British universities, including the John Innes Centre in Norwich, which houses the Sainsbury Laboratory. The strategy board of the Council contains executives from SmithKline Beecham, AgrEvo and Nestlé, all companies which we saw had representatives on other Task Forces and agencies; and Zeneca's employees sit on all seven specialist committees of the BBSRC.

George Monbiot's chapter entitled 'Silent Science: the Corporate Take-over of the Universities' will make your hair stand on end. The silence is imposed.

Schools

Big Business is not only interested in universities; it is interested in schools. Here it is prepared to put up money, but only for a profitable return. This can be achieved in several ways. The first is through the Private Finance Initiative, under which private capital investment is supplied to local authorities for building work which is then paid for over a period of years. This was designed to overcome an immediate shortage of funds resulting from the Government's determination to limit the Public Sector Borrowing Requirement. Before Labour came to power Alastair Darling, then shadow Chief Secretary to the Treasury, complained that 'apparent savings now could be countered by formidable commitment on revenue expenditure in years to come.' This did not stop him and his colleagues implementing the very policy he had criticised. Not only schools, but hospitals, prisons, police stations and other public buildings could be renovated or built at once, if private finance was attracted. Paying back the debts over the long term was someone else's problem. More will be said about this in the next section because it has most heavily affected the Health Service.

The second intervention of private capital into the schools is even more direct. In some areas standards in schools are particularly low and in need of extra resources. Such schools may be handed over to an 'action forum' to establish an Education Action Zone (EAZ). It is a requirement that this will include local business as well as parents, teachers and education authorities. Businesses are asked to put up money or goods and services supplemented by matching funds from Government. The actual management of the schools is taken over from the local authority by the action forum, which is often in effect run by the leading business company involved. Thus the EAZ in the London Borough of Lambeth is led by Shell; the EAZ in Wythenshawe, Manchester, by Manchester Airport; British Aerospace runs zones in Hull, Plymouth and Teesside; Tesco in Hereford; ICI in Blackburn; Cadbury Schweppes in Birmingham; Kelloggs in Salford and Trafford; McDonalds in Dudley, Somerset and Teesside. Serco is expected to get Leeds. One of the companies most frequently represented on EAZs is BT, which provides information technology with the recommendation that its own services should be used. Andersen Consulting, the giant multi-billion accounting firm, which we shall meet again later, has the advisory role in EAZs.

In addition to the EAZs a number of individual schools have been handed over directly to a private company. The first was Kings Manor School in Guildford, Surrey. Others have followed in Hackney and Islington. Nord Anglia, a company whose business is education management, was reported in the *Sunday Times* in February 1999 to have predicted that 200 state schools would be managed by private companies within five years. Stephen Byers announced in 1998 that the EAZs 'are the test bed for the education system of the twenty-first century.' In the United States, according to Naomi Klein in her book *No Logo*, over 1000 state schools had by 1998 already been contracted out to private companies. Schools in the United States are already saturated with advertising in the form of teaching packs, videos and TV programmes.

What then is in it for Business? The answer seems to be part prestige, part advertising for parents and children, part preparation of young people for what is called 'the world of work', part straight profit. England's well known private schools, the so-called 'public schools', are very profitable businesses. New Labour promised to deprive them of tax exemption as charities, but has yet to fulfil that promise. Some analysts (according to *Labour Research*, August 2000) estimate that the public sector contracts to run school services could be worth £1.6 billion. Companies involved in other PFI schemes are involved in school building as well as management. The Serco Group is a front runner with a one-time director whom we saw as Chief Executive Officer of the Government's Private Finance Panel. Serco is into hospitals, prisons, atomic weapons sites and, it hopes, air traffic control. Also involved in school building are WS Atkins engineering consultancy, which according to UNISON does not recognise trade unions, and Ensign (Tribal Group and Group 4) which has one executive, Sue Clifton, whom we saw earlier as an adviser on the Government's Youth Justice Board.

Preparation for the 'world of work' is becoming an ever more obvious aim of Business in Schools. Under the pretext of catering for the supposedly less academically inclined pupils, a break is being proposed at 14, when some will move in one year to GCSE and ultimately to higher education, while the others will follow a 'vocational course to meet the needs of pupils and the economy'. At one time employers had to finance their own training schemes through apprenticeships and day release. It is the ending of such schemes that accounts for the skill shortages about which employers have been complaining. Under New Labour's proposals the employers will have their training needs provided for them. The next step could be a return to the tri-partite system of grammar, technical and 'secondary modern', which comprehensive schooling replaced in the interest of greater equality.

Advertising is very obvious when a company runs the school. Gifts are announced on the radio and TV, even by the Secretary of State for Education. In the schools everyone knows the names of the donors; the logos are all around. Some companies in the UK, as in the USA, issue teaching packs and videos which contain advertising matter or slanted information, for example about the safety or healthy properties of their products. Disposable nappies, baby foods, sweets for energy, high fat foods, private cars, nuclear fuels may all be examples. The overall impact on children, and also on parents and staff, of this presence of business in schools, when the presence of trade unions or campaigning non-governmental orgnisations is absent, must be that the normal world is presented as a business world with business aims of competitive money-making paramount. Of course, children as they grow up are bombarded by this message on the screens of their televison sets which are often on all the time at home, while anything 'political' is kept off, and that can even exclude a Christian Aid TV advert calling for an end to Third World debt.

The Health Service

After education comes health in the proposed priorities of New Labour. Chronic lack of funds for buildings and for adequate staffing was the hallmark of the Health Service as it was of Education. Remedies were equally constrained by New Labour's commitment to hold down taxation. The solution once more lay in private finance. This was taken up by the New Labour Government with astonishing alacrity. Labour in opposition had warned against PFI in the Health Service. 'The future of services will be driven by the short-term priorities of the companies involved', as Harriet Harman, shadow Health Secretary warned in 1996, adding that 'NHS employees will be strangers in their own hospital – public servants in a privatised hospital'. Yet within a year, in July 1997, Alan Milburn, a new Treasury Minister, announced a review of the Private Finance Initiative, arguing that 'When there is a limited amount of public-sector capital available, as there is, it's PFI or bust'.

Within months, then, of its election to office the Private Finance Initiative had been reviewed and a Government report issued which wholly accepted the demands being made by the Confederation of British Industry. The Treasury's Private Finance Panel consisting mainly of civil servants was replaced with a Task Force drawn largely from Big Business, with David Steeds of Serco as Chief Executive under the chairmanship of the British Rail privatiser, merchant banker Adrian Montague. The Government report providing for this required the new Task Force 'to maintain frequent and active liaison with the private sector ...' with the 'addition of deal-making and project management expertise to be acquired initially from the private sector.' This, as we saw earlier, is where Mr. Robert Osborne came in who had already been recruited from Tarmac, one of the major builders of privately financed hospitals, and was retained by the new Government for six months before returning to Tarmac to carry on the good work.

A key recommendation of the Government report on the Private Finance Initiative was to the effect that financial commitments to private companies would have priority and payments promised would never be cut. The British Medical Association was appalled. In a devastating series of notes and editorials in the *British Medical Journal* the question was asked: 'Can the NHS afford the Private Finance Initiative?' (*British Medical Journal*, 17.7.99). Their worries were three fold. First, they asked what would be the effect of repayments of borrowed funds over the long periods of the proposed contracts, mainly for 25 to 35 years, but some for up to 60 years? 'The NHS', the BMA complained, 'could find itself with a facility which is obsolete in ten or twenty years' time, but for which it will still have to pay for thirty years or more.' In the case of University College London Hospital, one of the biggest ever private sector investments in the NHS, the costs of which doubled to £320 million since first announced, the NHS will have to repay the private contractor around £30 million a year for the next 32 years for leasing and other service charges. (LRD *Fact Service*, 16.09.99).

The second worry among all concerned with the NHS, and particularly of the Unions, represented by Unison, was the proposed down-sizing of the staffing of the new hospitals to be built under PFI. In order to ensure a profitable investment, numbers of beds and staff were to be cut back compared with the old hospitals that were being replaced. The argument was that better design could increase the take-up and through-put of patients. A series of studies by Declan Gaffney and Allyson Pollock flatly denied this and showed that some of the new designs had cut space around beds and in corridors to unworkable proportions. Moreover, according to Allyson Pollock, reporting to the BMA, the NHS Health Trusts running the first 14 hospitals to be built under the PFI will cut staffing by 10%-20% and reduce the number of beds by just under 4000, that is about a quarter of their current total. Coincidentally, when Health Minister Alan Milburn, in response to public outcry about continuing long waiting lists, announced in February 2000 an increase in the number of hospital beds, the target set was just 4000.

In spite of all the BMA's warnings, by April 2000, the Government announced that it had commissioned 34 privately financed hospital developments at a cost of £3.5 billions and at the same time six publicly funded developments to cost just £217 millions. Arthur Andersen, the consultants in a study of 29 PFI schemes, suggested that the saving of the tax payers' money would average about 17%. But Roger Tanner, consultancy director at NHS Estates, according to Unison, has suggested that private companies can only save this money through 'omissions, a smaller area, or lower specifications'. The Unions fear that another source of savings will be in the wages of the hospital porters, cleaners and other ancillary staff, already the worst paid in the country. A report issued in September 2000 from an independent think-tank, the King's Fund, criticised hospitals being built under PFI, on the grounds that they were not taking into account the needs of local people or the relation to other health services.

There was, moreover, a further snag, which was not so immediately evident, and was indeed often kept secret as 'commercially sensitive information'. In order to attract private funds, Health Trusts up and down the country found that they had to agree to closing, rather than renovating (at less cost) their old hospitals, and building a new hospital out of town on a green field site, where land could be taken over by the developer for other developments like out of town supermarkets as well as for the hospital's needs. This was the kind of 'sweetener' that , according to the Scottish *Sunday Mail* (10.01.99), had been offered to the companies building the new Edinburgh Royal Infirmary on the outskirts of the city and closing four of Edinburgh's old hospitals. George Monbiot, in his book already referred to so often here, tells at length the extraordinary story of the new Coventry hospital being built on a site at Walsgrave under a Private Finance Initiative, instead of renovating the three existing hospitals in the city, and against the expressed wishes of the Coventry Health Authority, the City Council, public opinion and even the local MP (a new Geoffrey Robinson, *after* resigning from the Government).

One further reason for Health Trusts and Local Authorities going for PFI funding is that this was seen as a way to obtain for a project a government subsidy which would otherwise not be available. One example of this was reported by UNISON from Dudley, where proposals for the Wordsley Hospital led to a threat of industrial action by the staff. The argument is complex. Before a private company is asked to bid for a project, an estimate is made of the likely cost as a public sector investment. This becomes the Public Sector Comparator (PSC), against which the private sector bidder's price is related. If the PFI is higher than the PSC, the government provides a subsidy, which is said to cover the risks which private capital are taking. But this so-called 'risk money' is spurious. The contract with the Treasury is guaranteed over a long period of years, and, as we have just seen, overspending is found from public funds. Questions about these peculiarities in the management of public funds were raised in the Public Accounts Committee of the House of Commons, and in 1999 a consultant was called in to make a report. This had become a serious matter because the number and range of PFI schemes encouraged by various Task Forces and other special units was growing exponentially.

Chapter Four
The Private Finance Initiative Everywhere

Not content with making profits from education and health, private finance has spread under the New Labour Government into a whole range of previously public services. In spite of the fact that since 1997 government finances have begun to show large surpluses, more and more private finance is being brought into public projects. Only 70 deals had been made when New Labour came into office, but the total now exceeds 250 valued at some £16 billion, due to rise in the next two years to £20 billion (and some estimates are much higher). The Andersen Consulting Group was commissioned in 1999 by the Treasury task force for PFI, whose Chief Executive Officer is, as we know, David Steeds, of the big PFI bidders the Serco Group, to review the working of PFI and address some of the criticisms made by the Public Accounts Committee of the House of Commons. Andersen Consulting gave an overall endorsement of PFI, which will not surprise anyone who read Paul Foot's article in the *London Review of Books* (02.11.00) about the two Andersen companies. His story gives a remarkable insight into the connections between New Labour and the British and American business world in which the giant accounting companies like Andersens exercise extraordinary power.

Andersen Consulting had offered its services free in 1993 to the Labour Party's Commission on Social Justice, set up by John Smith the then Labour Party leader. On the day that John Smith died, May 12 1994, Andersen Consulting announced that Patricia Hewitt, who had been Neil Kinnock's press officer and deputy chair of the Party's Social Justice Commission, was to be the new director of research at Andersen Consulting. This company in 1996 provided the entire team of New Labour prospective ministers with seminars on 'how to be an efficient minister'. More importantly, the year before in 1995 it had gained a multi-billion pound contract from the Government to store on computer all the national insurance benefit information under the new PFI, which would give all the intellectual property rights to Andersen Consulting. When the New Labour Government came to power in 1997, the Public Accounts Committee began to get worried about this and about the Government's failure to obtain any compensation for the endless delays in introducing the computerised system. Andersen Consulting was nonetheless named as the preferred bidders for advising on the Education Action Zones discussed in the previous section, with Graham Walker an Andersen senior partner on a New Labour Task Force .

Patricia Hewitt had meantime been elected Labour MP for Leicester West and was swiftly promoted as Economic Secretary to the Treasury and then Minister for e-business, in which capacity she had to defend the Government's support for the controversial Ilisu dam in Turkey. Arthur Andersen were the accountants for Balfour Beatty the British construction firm most involved in the dam project. There had been a long running quarrel between the British Government and Arthur Andersen, the partner firm of Andersen Consulting described in their own words as 'bound together'. This arose from the collapse of the DeLorean car empire in Northern Ireland, in which the Government had invested money on the recommendation of Arthur Andersen. Edward Heath, former Tory Prime Minister, was on Arthur Andersen's payroll at the time. In the event after legal action, a decree was issued banning Arthur Andersen from government work, but this did not evidently cover the partner firm Andersen Consulting (with all the same directors). Within six months of the election of a New Labour Government, the ban on Arthur Andersen was lifted on a 'negotiated settlement' of £18 million and in the year 2000 the two component Andersen companies were formally split up.

This is a fascinating story which Paul Foot was able to reveal, but the most alarming aspect of the advances of private capital into the country's infrastructure is the secrecy that surrounds the whole operation. According to the Treasury Private Finance Task Force Partnerships for Prosperity in 1997, 'preliminary discussions, on a confidential basis, might be held with … construction companies and developers, manufacturers; … bankers/financiers/insurers.' By the time those discussions are over it may be too late to mobilise public opinion, because changes would involve heavy compensation to those with whom discussions had been held. Persistent inquirers and whistle blowers have been warned off, but fortunately not too successfully.

The two Ministers made responsible in 1997 for preparing an

Information Disclosure Bill, David Clark and Nigel Griffiths, were sacked in 1998 for refusing to water down the European Union's Consumer Protection directive. The bill as it finally appeared from Jack Straw's office was a pale reflection of what New Labour had originally promised. What Stephen Byers, Secretary of State for Trade and Industry, has called 'unnecessary regulation' has been replaced by self-regulation. Health and safety inspectors have been reduced. This was particularly damaging in the building industry, not to mention food and agriculture. Thereafter, only 10% of major injuries at work were investigated and of these only 11% led to a prosecution. There was a subsequent 20% leap in deaths and serious injuries in construction work. (LRD *Fact Service* 11.11.99)

Roads, Railways, Prisons, Passports

Road building was promised by New Labour to be relegated to lower priority as part of an integrated transport policy which would give emphasis to railway and public transport. That is not quite how things have turned out. Motor traffic has continued to rise, investment in roads has been increased, but ideas of congestion charges and tolls have been dropped. Until the Hatfield rail disaster occurred, rail use had risen in face of growing road congestion. The efforts of the road hauliers' lobby, the Freight Transport Association, have not been in vain in their campaigns for ending restrictions on night journeys in residential areas, for larger lorries and for increased speed limits on country roads. All the super-market chains are, or were, members of the Association – Sainsbury, Safeway, Tesco, Asda, Marks & Spencer. Some road investment schemes which were expected to be shelved by New Labour have gone ahead.

George Monbiot has given an extraordinary example of the Birmingham Northern Relief Road proposal that was extremely unpopular with the communities it would disrupt and was opposed by Labour in opposition, including both Frank Dobson and John Prescott. When the New Labour Government nonetheless gave the project the go-ahead, explaining that the reasons for this policy change were 'commercially confidential', residents took the Government to court to see the contract. The judge ruled against them and they had to pick up the £50,000 legal bill. The same answer was given to the organisation Transport 2000, when they complained that privately built roads, which were said to be 15% cheaper than public roads, turned out after various hidden costs were revealed to be actually two and a half times more expensive.

The railway system is the most tragic of the many disasters of privatisation. It is said that the Channel Tunnel rail link would have cost £1 billlion, if publicly funded as was proposed in 1989. The private consortium that was asked to build the link was given £ 5.7 bn. of land and public money, according to *The Guardian* (04.06.98) and later in 1998 asked the Government for another £1.2 bn., and later got a £3.7 bn. loan as part of a £5.8 bn. refinancing loan. The story of Railtrack is peculiarly depressing. Gerald Corbett, Railtrack's chief executive, who resigned after the Hatfield rail crash, claimed that the railways had been 'ripped apart at privatisation', breaking it up into 25 train operating companies, four rolling stock companies and Railtrack. New Labour did nothing on being elected to re-nationalise the railway system, despite strong public demand for it, becoming especially strong after the Hatfield disaster.

Moreover, New Labour having apparently learned no lessons from Railtrack's failure, has continued with the plan to do to the London Underground the same as the Tories had done to British Rail, opposition to which probably won Ken Livingstone his victory in the London Mayoral election. Livingstone had described the bidders for the London Underground as 'a collection of capitalist scum as good as you could find'. One of them is the Bank of America, which not only financed the controversial Skye bridge over the Kyle of Lochalsh but also the A30 dual carriageway in Devon. The bank is the leading contender for the £1bn. Private Finance Initiative contract to update and operate London Transport's ticketing services. At the moment of writing, New Labour seems set on going ahead with the London Underground privatisation, in which a number of those whom we noted on Task Forces would be interested.

One of the many private profit innovations brought across the Atlantic from the USA to excite New Labour thinking was the proposal to put prison building and management into private hands. Jack Straw in Opposition had declared in 1996 that it is 'morally unacceptable for the private sector to undertake the incarceration of those whom the state has decided need to be imprisoned ...' Within a week of taking office, he had agreed 'to sign those contracts for privately financed jails that were already in the pipe-line'. A month later he renewed one private prison contract and signed for two new ones and a year on he told the Prison Officers' Association that all new prisons would be privately built and run. Five were already opened by April 2000 and four more were on the way. It is claimed that private prisons cost between 8% and 15% less to build, and less to run, but the Director-General of the Prison Service in England and Wales has stated that 'the great majority of the cost reduction comes from the payment of much lower wages and poorer conditions of staff working in the private sector'.

The results of the transfer of prisons to private management instanced by George Monbiot are dire. For example, and perhaps not surprisingly, one of these new private prisons, the Parc prison near Bridgend in Wales suffered eight minor riots and two suicides within a few weeks of completion. Prison Minister Joyce Quinn admitted in the House of Commons (12.2.98) that the prison lacked adequate work and training, drugs testing and visitor facilities. This only replicates stories from the United States, where prison building companies actually lobby state and federal government to introduce tougher penalties so as to increase the already swollen prison population. The Wackenhut Correction Corporation of the USA was reported in *The Observer* (20.08.96) to be one of the most controversial private prison operators in the US, with riots, stabbings, rapes and murders under its care. Nonetheless, the Home Office in August 1999 gave Premium Prisons, a Wackenhut subsidiary, contracts for prisons in Staffordshire and in Doncaster on top of those it already controls in Kilmarnock and Nottingham and the immigration centre at Gatwick.

The most famous or infamous story of a Private Finance Initiative failure was the collapse of the Passport Agency in the summer of 1999. The Siemens company was paid for this service according to the savings it delivered. These were achieved by heavy reductions of the staff. Delays built up and the introduction of a new computer system supposed to be a replacement for some of the staff ended in chaos. Thousands of people suffered disruption of their holidays and business plans. The Government did nothing to compensate them or to penalise the company. It was all blamed on the computer. We have heard that one before. Computers were also blamed in the handing over of National Insurance Recording to Andersen Consulting (yes, them again!) under a PFI scheme, which led to thousands of people losing their benefits. The original £1bn. plan to computerise Post Office Counters with the computer firm, ICL, through the PFI had to be abandoned after £130 million had already been paid.

Land and Water, Housing and the Supermarkets

When hospital building was put under the Private Finance Initiative, we saw that it was the land outside the city centres that the private investors wanted, so as to enrich their development. It has been the same with the building of supermarkets outside the city centres, and the same resistance of local communities has had to be overcome. In this case it is not a question of the takeover of public by private provision, but the displacement of small shops by large. Whenever a new supermarket is proposed the number of jobs that will be created is widely advertised. There is no mention of the number of jobs that will be destroyed. The New Economics Foundation has reported that £50,000 spent in a small shop creates one job, but £250,000 needs to be spent in a supermarket. This is one of the reasons why some goods are cheaper in the superstores and profits are much higher. There are of course other reasons – the monopoly power of their buyers and, less obviously, the land that they obtain planning permission to acquire.

George Monbiot gives detailed examples in his book of supermarket developments – from Brecon, Cheltenham, Romsey in Hampshire, Stockport in Greater Manchester, Pembury in Kent, Witney in Oxfordshire, Golden Hill in Bristol, Gerrards Cross in Buckinghamshire, Richmond in Surrey and most particularly from Southampton. In all these cases there was powerful local opposition to the development. This was not only from the rural communities losing their peace and quiet but most vociferously from the shop keepers and their customers in the town centres. It is everywhere the case that the opening up of an out-of-town superstore leads to the closing down of small shops in the towns. Mr Blair was arguing within a month of taking office that 'There are certain elements of the development of out-of-town shopping centres, for example, that I think really accord with what people want to do ...' (House of Commons 04.06.97). 'People' in this context are of course people with cars. The car parks that surround the stores use land that requires planning permission and involve the use of roads that the tax payer provides. For this reason John Prescott planned to introduce a tax on out-of-town parking in his White Paper on integrated transport. After some heavy lobbying by the superstores and some contributions to the Dome and to Labour Party funds, this proposal was dropped.

The spread of superstores across the face of Britain does not end with Tesco, Sainsbury, Safeway, Asda and Waitrose. In 1999 Walmart, the giant US retail chain, whose global sales exceed the combined total of all the British stores together, bought the British Asda chain for £6.7 billion, in spite of the fact that the Government had put a moratorium on new out-of-town stores. It was revealed by Gregory Palast in *The Observer* that Walmart had discussions with Tony Blair himself before its purchase and it has since become clear how it planned to side-step Government planning restrictions. *The Observer* newspaper in October 1999 discovered that Walmart was proposing to buy up entire out-of-town retail sites, demolish the shops and build larger stores using surrounding land where this was in the hands of the previous owners. It could do this, apparently, without having to obtain new planning permission. As the space available for such sites becomes limited, there is a monopolistic advantage for existing occupants, and as Walmart can bring prices down from its economies of large scale, the future of the shops in town becomes still further threatened; and Sainsbury's will have to look out.

The need for new houses in Britain is acute and there is a major argument about their location – on what are called 'brown sites', replacing old urban building, or on 'green sites', that is generally what has been designated in the past as the green belt surrounding urban areas. In this argument the lobbying by the construction industry has been intense. Something of this intensity was revealed in the cash for answers scandal in August of 1998, which involved Derek Draper boasting that he could get meetings for the chief executive of the House Builders' Federation with a Downing Street policy adviser. George Monbiot commented that this should not surprise anyone because the lobbying company employed by the Construction Federation and other building trades bodies was Lowe Bell Political, whose contact man just happened to have been previously the head of Tony Blair's briefing unit during the General Election campaign of 1997.

John Prescott's junior ministers at the Department of the Environment, Transport and the Regions seem to have seen part of their job as 'creating a climate in which the [construction] industry can do well – like unblocking the Private Finance Initiative ...' and 'improving the effectiveness of trade associations and other industry groups' as Nick Raynsford averred in the 1998 *Annual Report* of the Department. Richard Caborn went further. In a Department Progress Report on *Modernising Planning* issued in April 1998, he announced that preparation of Britain's regional planning should be 'business led'. 'We propose to produce a guide for business on how to become more closely involved in the planning process.'

The results of this modernised planning were perhaps to be expected. In both the Forest of Dean and in the Peak District National Park earlier Labour promises were abandoned. The amount of new quarrying for aggregate was to have been reduced and more old material recycled, but that is not what has happened. The record under New Labour of the authorisation of green field sites for development in Newbury, Sutton Coldfield and elsewhere, despite negative planning inspectors' reports, augurs ill for the final decisions on the locations for the new housing that must be built in the next 20 years. Under PFI terms and conditions it will always be cheaper and more profitable to build on green fields. One of George Monbiot's New Labour 'Fat Cats', Lord de Ramsey, former Chairman of the Environment Agency, has shown the way, by selling part of his Cambridgeshire estate for the construction of 3000 new houses, doubling the size of the village of Ramsey.

New Labour's policies on the water industry were already laid down by the Tories' privatisation policies. Excess profits were subjected to a special one-off 'windfall profit' tax, much of which was passed on to the consumers. Once again it was the development of the land, in this case the lands surrounding the water supplies and reservoirs, that the new owners had their eyes on. The subsequent strict limits on price increases imposed by the regulator Ofwat has led to a number of water companies – Wales and Yorkshire in particular – looking at ways of splitting their assets and selling off the water supplying operation to consumers through some form of mutual organisation. There are no water company chairmen on New Labour's list of 'fat cats', possibly because several of them are the heads of large French companies. Some water companies were heavily criticised by the Environment Agency for inadequate river control schemes during the floods of the autumn of 2000, but then the Environment Agency is well represented, as we saw, among the 'fat cats'.

The Great Energy Fix

One of the most controversial issues facing New Labour on its election to office was the future of the coal mining industry and the share of coal in the generation of electricity. In the event, the coal industry was allowed to dwindle, but not quite to disappear in the face of a massive building programme of gas-fired power stations. There were no 'fat cats' from coal but plenty from oil and gas and powerful ministerial support. The most astonishing story concerning the energy industry was told by Gregory Palast in *The Ecologist*, to which reference was made in our discussion about Peter Mandelson's friends. Somehow, some markets had to be found for British coal, despite its high price relative to gas for power generating, while still satisfying the demands of the electricity companies for gas. The major company involved was PowerGen, a part US company, which by 1998 was fixing 85% of the price bids in the 'power pool' and wanted to extend its influence by taking over East Midlands Electricity. The Government in the person of Margaret Beckett, Secretary of State for Trade and Industry, turned down this merger and had slapped a moratorium on new gas-fired generating plants (albeit after several had already got through). PowerGen was also interested in a merger with a US power group, Houston Industries, which Mrs Beckett was questioning.

According to Palast, Geoffrey Robinson as Paymaster General came up with the solution to the problem of satisfying coal and gas. He appears to have been 'helped' by three back-channel orders from the Clinton administration in Washington. Internal US Embassy files showed that the orders to Blair regarding the UK electricity system were:

- 'to keep a lid on Labour's proposed 'windfall profit' tax on US companies which already owned half the system;'
- 'to get this Mrs. Beckett out of the way of several American merger targets;'
- 'to let US power companies build gas-fired power plants in the UK.'

What Robinson added to make a deal was that these three demands should be agreed if Powergen would take 25 million tonnes of coal, something Mrs Beckett had not suggested. As Palast tells the story, Robinson met PowerGen's Chief Executive Officer, Ed Wallis, in June 1998; Margaret Beckett was replaced by Peter Mandelson at the DTI on July 27; Mandelson agreed PowerGen's takeover of East Midland Electricity on September 22; PowerGen signed contracts for 25 million tonnes of British coal on September 23; and within a short time a series of waivers on gas plants were issued followed by the total removal of the moratorium.

This was not, however, the end of the matter. There was still the question of PowerGen's American merger interests. One day in July 1998, when Mandelson was still Blair's Minister without Portfolio, the British tabloid press had run a startling story with pictures of Mandelson dancing all night in Rio with a young man named Fabrizio and, in smaller print, that the Brazilians were upset because Mandelson had given the thumbs up on Brazilian TV to Brazil's President, Henrique Cardoso, who was fighting a tough election battle for re-election in face of a collapsing economy. This gesture of support may just have turned the balance as indicating Euro-American leaders' support for a safe pair of hands, and have given Cardoso his squeaky thin majority. There was much more to it even than that.

Once Cardoso was safely installed, the US Treasury gave the nod and Brazil's currency dropped by 40%. The financial institutions led by the IMF and the World Bank moved in to demand in exchange for loans and credits that financial and economic 'reforms' were introduced for 'flexible production', including the reduction of salaries, benefits and pensions, increased working hours and reduced job stability and employment. Mandelson's mission was not so much concerned with these reforms as with the results of the collapse of the

Brazilian currency. At low rates for the Brazilian Real to the £sterling and the US$, British Gas picked up the Sao Paolo Gas company for a song; US power companies got the Rio and Sao Paolo electricity companies and a pipe line. Perhaps the whole samba dancing story was deliberately manufactured to draw attention away from what Mandelson was doing with and not without his portfolio.

Gregory Palast truly believes that there was a real project hatched out between Clinton and Blair, which involved US capital expanding in Britain – PowerGen and Entergy (London Electricity), Esso, Monsanto, Walmart, Wackenhut Prisons, McDonalds, Kelloggs, Murdoch too (since he is a US citizen). The conditions for that involvement were de-regulation, privatisation, a flexible work force, information technology and international business cooperation. The terms of the involvement were being worked out by the Trans-Atlantic Business Dialogue (TABD), to which Blair and Clinton swore allegiance at their meeting in Birmingham in May 1998. The secret Implementation Plan of TABD dated October 1999, according to Palast, targets 33 key environmental, consumer and worker protection laws in selected nations to defeat or defang.

The Trans-Atlantic Business Dialogue Plan makes it clear, however, that this does not apply only, or even primarily, to industry. Robert Reich, the Project's so-called 'sound-bite philosopher', has set out what he supposes to be the basis for the Blair-Clinton programme, in his book *The Work of Nations*. The new world, he believes, will belong to the manufacturers of ideas; the dirty business of actually making things will be left to declining or developing nations of routine producers.

What that means for Britain will be the subject of the next chapter.

Chapter Five
A Manufacturing or Service Economy?

The story that has run through this little book so far is the story of the takeover of Britain – turning Britain into what George Monbiot has called *The Captive State*. But the story can also be seen to be of the take-over of a government, through the 'Captive Party'. It appears that C(c)apital has moved in to take over L(l)abour in the whole range of activities in the British political economy, not just in the personnel of the government apparatus of departments and committees, but in all the functions of traditional government and in these ways to make L(l)abour more than ever subordinate to C(c)apital. Conservatives always used to put their people into key positions when they were in government. Labour in government in the past did the same with its own people, though very unwisely to a much lesser extent. This time, as we have seen, it is not Labour people at all who are in the positions of power, but the leaders of the largest concentrations of capital in the country.

But this is not all that has happened. A much bigger transformation has been taking place. This has two aspects. The first is that through privatisation, the Private Finance Initiative and other means, all public affairs, which have been established over many years, even centuries, as *res publica*, matters of public health and safety and the preservation of common knowledge, to be determined by public discussion and debate, have been submitted to the private calculation of profit and loss. The second is that Capital has moved into this domain because it is seen to be more profitable, now and in the future, than the areas of industry and commerce in which it was previously engaged. The corollary of the invasion by private capital of the public services which we have been observing is its retreat from mining and manufacturing industry. The facts of this retreat are hardly in doubt as far as Britain is concerned.

The Decline in Manufacturing
When Mrs Thatcher became Prime Minister in 1979 there were 7.5 million jobs in manufacturing, mining and other productive industry in the UK. By 1994 the number was down to 4.2 million. The figure

rose to 4.4 million in 1998 but was down to 4.2 million again at the end of 1999. Another 100,000 jobs were lost in the year 2000 and the TUC has estimated that a further 100,000 will be lost in 2001. This loss of 3.5 million jobs in industry over the 20 years has, of course, been made up by an increase of jobs in services. This increase amounts over this period to some 5 million, bringing the total to over 18.5 million in 2000, over four times those in production; but since a large proportion of the new service jobs are part-time, replacing full-time jobs in production, actual employment will hardly have increased (assuming that two part-time jobs equals one full time). The New Labour election claim is that a million new jobs have been created since May 1997, but the high proportion of these which are part-time and the continuing loss of full-time employment means that this number should be scaled down accordingly.

There are a number of reasons which explain the decline of industry in Britain, apart from Mrs Thatcher's shop-keeping inheritance and her determination to destroy the miners.

The first is that over a long period of time, many centuries, the number of people and the hours that they worked simply to meet the needs for survival, food, clothing, shelter, safety have been steadily reduced. With the agricultural and industrial revolutions of the Eighteenth Century, mechanisation of production enormously reduced the numbers and hours required, and made available for large numbers of people, and not just a tiny elite, the free time for leisure activities. As this time increased, so the provision of services began to catch up on the necessary supply of goods. More and more people had some discretionary spending power, not concerned with meeting essentials. Between 1911 and 1990 the proportion of the occupied population in Great Britain engaged in Government activity and Services rose from 25% to 43% of the total and those in Transport and Distribution rose from 20% to 26%. Most of these increases, moreover, took place during the 1980s and 90s, so that the total non-productive proportion (if transport is called non-productive) is today over two-thirds of the total. And we have just seen evidence to suggest that this may now be increasing further.

Even given the long historical trend, it is necessary, therefore, to explain the very rapid decline in manufacturing and the increase in

41

service employment over the last two decades. The first explanation must be the rise of manufacturing output overseas, and especially of cars and electronic products, from Japan, Korea and South East Asia. Producers in these lands have been able to combine the use of advanced technology with relatively cheap labour. To some extent and for a time, the location of their production was actually moved into the UK to take advantage of local markets in Britain and Europe. When established here, their high levels of labour productivity have raised output but without increasing employment. We have so far been measuring the decline of manufacturing and other industry in terms of employment, but even if we measure the contribution of industry to the national product, that too has been declining. Indeed the output of manufacturing has scarcely risen in real terms over the decade of the 1990s. Only oil and gas output from the North Sea showed an increase that was in excess of that of national output as a whole, and that has ceased. It is the value of the output of services that has been leaping ahead, accounting for a historical record run in economic growth over the decade.

A part of this investment was in information services, although in real terms this was not as much as the Stock Market prices suggested. The new information technology and the spread of the internet and with it of a prodigious increase in advertising has attracted great quantities of capital. Much of it is concerned with how we shop and what we buy in the shops, but increasingly what you can find on the internet concerns precisely the private sector's interest in health, particularly health insurance, in education and private sources of information and instruction, in old age and pension provision, in every kind of holiday and recreational services, and above all in the media. It is not surprising that we saw that one of New Labour's key Task Forces was the Creative Industries Task Force, with major Labour donors like Alan McGee from Creation Records, Lord Puttnam of Anglia Television, and Lord Waheed Alli of Planet 24 on it. In fact the media and the advertising world are particularly well represented among Labour's big donors. We have already listed other Labour lords from the media – Lords Bernstein, Bragg, Gavron, Hollick, Macdonald. Advertising is equally to the fore among Labour financial supporters – in the lobbyist, Paul Adamson, and advertising tycoons Leslie Butterfield, Felix Dennis, and Frank Lowe. None of this should be regarded as at all surprising. This is now where the money is.

The other and most recent explanation for the decline in manufacturing in the UK has been the high value of the £ sterling in world trade exchanges. Many British manufactures – motor cars, textiles and footwear, machinery and chemicals – have simply been priced out of the world market. As a result, either exports have collapsed or trans-nationally operating firms have moved their plants from the UK to Europe, the USA or even back overseas. We have seen this exodus in the motor industry, in the cut-back of Fords at Dagenham, General Motors/Vauxhall at Luton, BMW/Rover at Longbridge, in steel making at Corus in Scunthorpe, South Wales and the North East, in textiles and pipes in the East Midlands, in electronics in Sunderland. Since New Labour came to office in 1997, there has been a massive outflow of capital from the UK. The net outflow of private direct investment, that is of exports of capital minus imports, has risen from £6 billion in 1997 to over £100 billion in 2000. Some of this rise can be offset against an increase in portfolio investment in the UK, as in the case of the Mannesmann purchase by Vodaphone, but by no means all.

As a corollary of expanding UK overseas investment there has been a decline of investment at home, particularly in manufacturing. While private business investment each year in the production industries actually declined between the years 1995 and 2000, from over £30 billion to around £27 billion, investment in services doubled over the same period from £42 billion to £84 billion. No better example could be given of the trend for Britain to become a service economy. The Private Finance Initiative is not a small part of this investment in services, in roads, prisons, hospitals, schools etc., some £16 billion worth of deals having been completed by the end of 1999.

Such a sharp decline in the production and exports of goods has its effect on the UK balance of payments with other countries, goods having ever since 1945 played a larger role than services. Between 1997 and 2000 the deficit on trade in goods (that is exports less imports) rose from £12 billion to an estimated £28 billion, while the positive balance on services, which generally helps to pay for the trade deficit, actually declined from £12 billion to £11 billion. Nor, despite the increase in overseas investment, did this bring in very much extra investment income from abroad. The overall result is that whereas New Labour inherited a positive balance on the foreign current account of some £6 billion in 1997, an overall deficit of £12 billion is expected to have been run up in 2000. Another way of saying this is that instead of British capital lending £6 billion a year overall, it was borrowing £12 billion.

'Reform' and the Free Movement of Capital

British capital as a whole is evidently borrowing in the short term to invest long term. This state of affairs cannot obviously continue; it is presumably a function of the high £. This is because a high value of the £ in relation to other currencies, particularly the $ and the euro, while it makes British exports dearer and fatally uncompetitive, allows those who hold £s to buy up plants and factories on the cheap in the $ and euro zones. While it lasts, the effect on British manufacturing industry is lethal. Is this overseas investment fling by holders of capital assets in Britain, then, the reason why the value of the £ has been kept so high for so long, when it has been a disaster for British industrial production and employment? It must be part of the reason, but the chief reason has to be found in the management of British interest rates.

Interest rates in Britain since New Labour came to power have been set by the Bank of England under Government guidance. During this time they have been persistently about twice the level of those obtaining in Europe and generally in line with those set in the USA by Mr Greenspan. A relatively high rate of interest obviously attracts those with money to lend and, other things being equal, they will lend to persons and organisations in the country where the highest rates obtain. But that has the effect of raising the value of that country's currency. Britain under New Labour has therefore had a regime of high interest rates and a high £. But why? The Government's guidance to the Bank of England is that it must keep the rate of inflation in the UK down to certain levels that the Government sets from time to time. This is the key requirement. A relatively high rate of interest is evidently needed to keep inflation down in the UK, because there is a tendency for it to get out of hand when output and employment are high.

All that we are here discussing is part of what is called globalisation. Not only are goods and services free to move all over the world, with certain restrictions still imposed by governments to protect their agriculture and some other industries, but movements of capital are free too. This is why changes in interest rates immediately affect capital flows and result in higher or lower currency values. The freeing of capital movements was one of Mrs Thatcher's gifts to the British people. It was one part of the doctrine of monetarism to which she and her friend President Reagan were devoted as good followers of Professor Milton Friedman. The value of money was made sacrosanct; it should not be allowed to depreciate, that is to say that the price of goods and services in money terms should not be permitted to rise. Employment didn't matter. Inflation became the first enemy; it had to be stopped; and the main cause of inflation, according to Professor Friedman, was Government spending.

A radical political programme was launched by Reagan and Thatcher under the title of neo-liberalism, and it is this programme which New Labour has been committed to continuing. Its chief elements are freedom for national and international movements of capital, as well as of the supply of goods and services, low levels of inflation and reductions in the expenditure and market intervention by government. Earlier aims of government such as full employment and a more just society were set aside. All that we have seen in earlier chapters concerning the increasing involvement of business in managing the economy and of private profit in place of public provision follows from the pursuit of this radical programme. Mr Blair calls it 'reform'; and if it means the destruction of British industry that is an unfortunate temporary adjustment on the way to Mr Blair's vision of a 'dynamic modern economy' as capital moves freely into its new sources of profitability.

The Victory of Capital over Labour

What the reform programme meant from the beginning was a massive onslaught on the trade unions, both through raised levels of unemployment – to a rate of over 10% in the early 1980s and early 1990s – and through fiercely restrictive legislation. Without this and the defeat of the miners, it would have been much harder for the switch of capital to take place from industry to services. There were other crucial factors making possible such a major victory of capital over labour as we have been seeing. These were both political and technological developments. The Reagan and Thatcher reforms did not arise by parthenogenesis from the fertile brain of Professor Friedman. They had a long fertilisation from evolutionary changes.

The first was the growing weakness and final collapse of the Soviet Union under the burden of the arms race culminating in the destruction of Gorbachev's attempts to democratise the Communist institutions. This rendered possible the Reagan-Thatcher termination of the post-war settlement between capital and labour. The overthrow of Labour in the UK was not just to be seen in the electoral defeats of the 1980s but even more clearly in the smashing of the Unions during the 1990s. Between 1988 and 1998 TUC membership fell from 10.4 million to 6.6 million. During, and for a time after the Second World War, the Soviet experiment remained a beacon of hope for many working people. The Khrushchev revelations destroyed that hope. Many despaired, and others were confused and abandoned politics. But the Soviet bogey remained in the fears of capitalists as well as of social democrats, encouraging them to support full employment and the welfare state. When these fears were finally put to rest, jobs and welfare could be cut back. In this new world, some from the Left even changed sides. The Blair cabinet is resplendent with Stalinist and Trotskyist renegades. Even more important, the masters of capital felt free to proclaim themselves and to enrich themselves as they had never dared to do before. The lists of new millionaires which are published in the press from time to time and the extraordinary array of 'fat cats' which George Monbiot has presented to us would never have been possible without the prior collapse of the Soviet Union.

It is not being suggested that Britain in the 1950s, 60s and 70s was a land of milk and honey with no economic problems, a prosperous manufacturing and mining industry, where unions and management bargained freely, with no foreign balance of payments deficits, while governments maintained full employment and withdrew from Empire avoiding costly wars. It was only a bit like that. There really were jobs for all and the slumps and inequalities of the years before the Second World War had been alleviated. That such economic improvement had been possible was not just because the capitalist class had to make concessions in face of a Soviet alternative. It had much more to do with the manufacturing technology of the time. Manufacturing and other productive industries dominated the economy and they were based on large scale runs of output from large fixed product lines – the Ford technology. To make these possible the market had to be widened, and that meant raising wages so that purchasing power was expanded into a mass market. The corollary was a labour force organised in mass unions, engaged in centralised wage bargaining. Industrial workers saw themselves as a unified class and supported a Labour Party, whose main task was seen to be maintaining full employment, the National Health Service and social security in temporary unemployment, illness and old age.

What chiefly ended this era was not Reagan, Thatcher and Professor Friedman or the demise of the Soviet Union, but a revolution in industrial technology. There were two aspects to this: the first was the spread and sophistication of automatic processes in production, wiping out whole swathes of skilled workers; the second was the reduction in the size of plants and the scale of runs that the new computerised information systems made possible. Small plants with flexible production and small runs meant the end to the need for a mass market as well as the end to massed workers in mass unions. Wage bargaining was decentralised. The trade unions lost power as small plants grew up all over the country often in areas with no previous tradition of union organisation. The Labour Party lost its roots and ceased to be seen by workers increasingly employed in services and not in productive industry as their natural Party. It was Mr Blair's project to adjust the Party to a new kind of economy. The dream of a fundamental shift in power from the rich to the poor achieved by mass action had to be abandoned. The New Labour appeal was to the individual, freeing everyone who can do so to get rich through developing the new technology, and that was bound to mean especially for those who were already rich to get richer. But will it work?

Can the 'Reform' work?
That is now the question as capital moves from large scale to small scale operation and increasingly from manufacturing to services. We

have already noted the mounting deficit on the balance of foreign payments resulting from the falling off of exports of goods (£172 billion in 1997; £166 billion in 1999; may be better in 2000) and the inexorable rise in imports (£184 billion in 1997; £192 billion in 1999; estimated £210 billion in 2000); and we noted that this was not balanced by an increase in net income from services, although there was some rise in net investment income from the expanded overseas investment. If the balance of foreign payments could be improved, there remain problems about a primarily service based economy, even with all the advances of information technology.

The first arises from the fact that all successful economies in the past have enjoyed a very wide range of activities so that no single one becomes predominant and therefore at risk from changes in demand. By contrast, a heavy predominance of primary commodities in the production and exports of many of the developing, ex-colonial economies has been the chief cause of their difficulties when demand for them has fallen. Is it any wiser to rely almost wholly on a service economy, however highly technical it may be?

The success of a mainly service economy today depends on the progress of the information revolution. The initial euphoria which gave enormous expected capital gains to almost any company announcing that it was going to provide services on line has largely evaporated. There is none the less little doubt that information services will be central to the economies of the future. More and more goods are sold as part of a complete package of hardware and software services. As the actual cost of the hardware is steadily reduced, it is inevitable that an increasing part of our spending will be on support services and on our health, education and leisure pursuits. That is the reason for the huge invasion we have been looking at of private capital into these areas. The shift of investment, which we have noted, is not just of capital from manufacturing and productive industries into services, but of private capital into what was the public domain.

There is absolutely no doubt about the profitability of investment in these areas. This is not only because of the extremely favourable terms on which the switch is being made. We have seen some of these in the arrangements made for PFI where lands were included for development, but there have apparently been many other 'windfall profits' in the deals that have been made under PFI. Following questions asked in the House of Commons by a member of the Commons Public Accounts Committee, it was revealed that only in one quarter of the PFI deals was a contractual right agreed for the public sector to share in such profits, and even where this was agreed and such profits accrued few payments have been made. Quite apart from such windfalls the terms of the deals that we looked at gave long-term profits to private investors far in excess of the costs that would have been incurred by public investment.

Profitability and Inequality

But this is only a part of the story. By getting in at the beginning of the information revolution in the service economy private capitalists can establish an unassailable position from which it will be hard for advocates of public provision to dislodge them. The objection that must be made to so much private capital involvement is that the requirement to put profitability first, while not necessarily making for a less efficient service, is likely to mean putting the needs of those who can pay most before those who are less able to pay. The whole process of privatisation has gone hand in hand with increasing inequalities in our society. This is not only because of the obscene payments made to the 'fat cats' in the privatised utilities and in the big companies associated with them, but because of the fundamental logic of capital accumulation. To see how this works in practice we must turn to look in detail at the arguments which have for so many years been advanced for preferring public over private provision in the common services we all need in matters of health, education, welfare, transport, housing and town and country planning. Can private capital plus the new technology overturn those arguments?

The dangers for the whole British economy arising from increasing inequalities have been highlighted by a group of Cambridge economists in a special issue on 'Social Justice and Economic Efficiency' of the *Cambridge Journal of Economics* (vol.24, no.6, November 2000). Contrary to all the arguments of the government economists over the last two decades, strict economic policies and deregulating markets in the name of economic efficiency have not been the cause of the long period of economic growth. The downward trend of import prices – oil and other commodities – combined with the strong £ provide a more convincing explanation. But this has meant a rising deficit on the balance of payments and a recent very low growth in productivity. Since 1996, as we have seen, the difficulties have worsened. Prices have in fact risen twice as fast as productivity and earnings three times as fast. The Government is living, so the Cambridge economists argue, on borrowed time as well as borrowed money, which is perhaps why the date of the next General Election has been advanced. In the concluding words of the editorial from three of the economists, Michael Kitson, Ron Martin, and Frank Wilkinson,

> 'The twin neo-liberal notions that higher incomes are required to motivate the rich – whilst lower wages and cuts in benefits are needed to get the poor to work – have been used to justify a more unequal distribution of income, and cuts in taxes on higher incomes. The adoption of these views as the conventional wisdom has lifted responsibility for unemployment and poverty from the government and shifted it onto the jobless and the poor themselves.'

The facts are not in doubt. According to the tables published by the Government Statistical Service in *Economic Trends* (April 2000) on 'The effects of taxes and benefits on household income', the poorest fifth of the households saw their post-tax income drop from 1997-8 to 1998-9, from a share of 7% to 6% of the total (it had been 10% in 1978) while the richest fifth enjoyed a gain over the same period from 44% to 45% (it was 36% in 1978).

That is clear enough, but we still have to understand why a shift from public to private services should generate such inequalities, and whether and for how long it can work.

Chapter Six
Private Profit or Public Provision?

It has become increasingly accepted that one can buy anything these days – from babies to a cure for cancer, from a beautiful nose to longevity, from sex to sunshine, from pure water to healthy food, from painless travel to a stress-free office. It is the business of the advertising agencies to convince us of this beneficence of the market. Of course, if you have enough money, it is true that all these good things in life can be bought. But some things come pretty costly. Fresh air to live in, totally unpolluted, is a good example. You would need an estate the size of Chatsworth to guarantee that. You could take a helicopter and fly to your other estate in the Bahamas for the sunshine. But for everything else, even the super rich have to rely on the care and vigilance of others – food, water, child care, health, education, housing, and safety from many dangers. Such care and vigilance can also be bought, although again it comes expensive with your own farm and gardens, water, nannies, private medicine, personal tutors, stately homes, guards and alarm systems, and the work done on the estate. But the chain of commercialisation lengthens because much has to be bought in from outside. The question then still arises whether private profit or public service is the better guarantee.

For everyone except the super rich, there is little choice. A few can afford private child care and health care and private schooling and large houses and gardens, with alarm systems, but much more has still to be bought in the market or obtained from public provision. Most people are entirely dependent on the market and on what the advertisers say, for their food and water, medicines, housing, transport, working conditions, sports and holidays. Health and education are still largely provided for by public services, but we have seen how far public provision is being eroded here by the initiatives of private finance. Protection against the spread of disease, against contamination of food and water, against crime and violence, against flood and fire, and against hostile action has been the historic responsibility of public authorities. To these basic public duties there came to be added in the last century responsibility for positive measures of health care, welfare, housing and education, postal and other communications, road, rail and air transport . What we have seen in the last chapters is that all these responsibilities are now being transferred step by step from public provision to private profit-making companies, even to encompass crime prevention, the management of prisons and many aspects of the defence of the realm.

The Question of Motivation

The BSE and E Coli outbreaks, the doubts about genetically modified crops and additives in our food, the breakdown of our flood and storm defences, the failures in our schools, the lengthening of waiting lists in hospitals, and the neglect of road and rail safety have all shown that public provision has become increasingly inadequate. Is the answer then to switch to the private sector? It is said that private enterprise is more efficient than public, because of the consciousness of costs that the force of competition ensures, which implies the threat of the sack for failure and the prospect of handsome monetary rewards for successful achievement. By contrast, public provision relies on moral responsibility for failure and a warm sense of duty well done in the event of success. How are to judge between such different motivations?

Costs and particularly labour costs are the central target of private company accounting, because they have the most manageable effect on the bottom line, which is profit. In most cases where private finance has been preferred to public provision, the reason given has been respective costs, to get so-called 'value for money'. But in several cases which we looked at earlier, reductions in staffing and even in space suggested that value was not the same. In other cases costs had been reduced because land could be developed outside the main project. There is always a danger with a non-profit enterprise running on a grant, that bureaucracy proliferates, the motivation to improve weakens, slackness creeps in. But against that must be reckoned the stresses and errors arising from understaffing, the tensions of competition overlaying the benefits of cooperation, the cutting of corners and the risks taken to achieve monetary targets.

There can be no doubt that tests and targets provide valuable checks of performance, but they are not necessarily the best form of testing for general popular satisfaction when they concentrate on monetary measures. Consumer satisfaction in the market is tested by whether consumers buy or don't buy among alternative similar products/services. In many public services being privatised there is in effect no choice, and making some competition available is not at all satisfactory. The hospital market has been a mess; rival telephone and gas suppliers have involved much digging up of roads not paid for by the companies; school choice is encouraging a damaging form of competition and the development of a two-tier school system. The splitting up of the railways did not really provide a choice of routes, but delivered disasters. There are always other measures for testing performance, in terms of time and other resources used, instead of relying on profitability. Losses mean bankruptcy and the failure of the service, loss of jobs and no lessons learned by trying to understand the reasons for failure. Motivation is not necessarily improved, nor is accountability clearly established.

The displacement of trade unions and especially their shop stewards from a central role in production and management processes has raised big questions about the actual economic efficiency of the private profit making company. The era of collaboration between management and unions in joint production committees during and immediately after the Second World War was followed by a period of sharpening struggle between labour and capital in industry during which major gains were made by organised labour towards controlling the terms and conditions of its employment, and even extending to some influence on investment decisions. This was all ended with the Thatcher onslaught on the unions and the spread of flexible production. At the same time, new ideas of individual and group worker participation in production spread from Japan encouraged by the success of Japanese industry. Their application in the UK has been half-hearted. What is left behind is an unhappy mix of cynicism in the workforce and high handedness in management. Unfortunately, this experience is to be found equally in the public sector, and particularly in NHS hospitals, as in the private sector. But remedies in the public sector can be more easily achieved by political action.

The Causes of Inequalities

Some kind of response to popular demand in public service provision has historically been supplied in a political democracy by the choice of programmes offered by political parties at elections. This has been most effective at local level where there might be sharp divisions between parties, as for example over the sale of council houses or the subsidy for public transport. Central government restrictions on local government spending under recent Conservative governments, continued by New Labour, have greatly reduced this form of responsibility to public opinion. The pressure from big companies upon governments to reduce the taxes they and their top managers pay, under threat of withholding and even withdrawing their investment, has placed a much greater weight of taxation on the great mass of middle level incomes. Since it appears to be in what is called 'Middle England' that the outcome of national elections is decided, so it is that all the political parties promise tax cuts to win votes, although opinion polls suggest that considerable majorities would prefer more public spending.

There is a clear difference in the effect on the distribution of resources between richer and poorer members of society which comes from private as opposed to public service provision. Since opinion polls may reflect a wider and poorer constituency than those who trouble to vote, governments may find themselves neglecting the interests of the poorer members of society in reducing public provision which depends on taxation. The main reason for the difference in the effect on income groups of public and private services is that public services have to be available to all, whereas private services will only be available to those who can afford them. If public services deteriorate because of reduced government spending, as they very obviously have done, those who can afford to will switch to the private sector. A vicious circle results. As more people make the switch, they are less willing to pay their taxes, public spending is further cut and still more people make the switch. The results are obvious in health, education, pensions, transport and recreational facilities.

The most serious result of this process has taken place in relation to pensions. The steady erosion in the value of the state pension has driven more and more of those who could afford to make the necessary savings to enter into private pension schemes. This has itself had two knock-on results. The first is that the New Labour Government, balking at the cost of restoring the value of the universal pension, has proposed to replace it with a means tested scheme for the poor. As David Donnison has argued in a companion publication to this one, 'Working people know that services designed specially for the poor always ended up as poor services'. John Grieve Smith in another companion pamphlet has shown just how damaging New Labour's espousal of means tested welfare is for poorer families, and most especially for the aged.

The second result of the switch to private pension schemes has been that large numbers of people have been swindled. This was not only the case of the infamous Maxwell pension fund, the Barlow-Clowes failure and now of the losses faced by Equitable Life savers, but other companies have been censured for mis-selling of pensions. These have included two with representatives on the various Government Task Forces, which we listed earlier. John Bowman, a director of Commercial Union, a company which was named and shamed by the Treasury for possible mis-sold pensions, is actually on the board of the Occupational Pensions Regulator, which is supposed to protect pensioners from being exploited. Even where there is no misappropriation involved, the administrative costs of private pensions can take up to 25% of the contributions, compared with 1% in the case of the universal state pension.

The switch to private pensions has given a bonanza to the pensions industry at the expense of the poorest members of our society. The argument that the rich could easily afford to make their own private savings and should not be subsidised out of the taxation of the less affluent can easily be dealt by raising the tax rates of the rich. Yet this is not proposed in New Labour policies, and the rich continue to pay a smaller proportion of their incomes in tax than do the poor, taking into account indirect taxes, such as VAT, as well as income tax. Inequality is built into New Labour's proposals for reliance on private pension schemes, just as it is throughout the whole programme of privatisation and Private Finance Initiatives.

If the Cambridge economists whom we quoted earlier are right, it is not only a matter of social justice to correct the trend towards greater inequalities in the UK, but a matter of economic efficiency. The system isn't working and they appeal for a complete policy reverse, requiring a new attitude in government to collective bargaining with organised labour. They point to 'other countries which achieved a degree of social cohesion, high quality training and rapid retraining which created a highly skilled and flexible labour force, while high social welfare standards and full employment reduced labour market uncertainty and resistance to change. The resulting high rates of productivity made inflation more easily contained, and this in turn increased competitiveness and economic performance.'

We can look at this claim again, but the picture drawn could hardly be more different from Mr. Blair's project of 'providing the most business friendly environment in the world', which has enriched the rich and impoverished the poor, as we can see from the tables published in *Economic Trends* in April 2000 which we quoted at the end of chapter five.

Planning and Consultation

The very word 'planning' has become anathema since the failure of the type of state planning adopted in the Soviet Union. Yet big companies plan all the time and governments have to make plans. We have seen, however, how far private initiatives have been able to bypass the plans of local authorities, especially in relation to land use. It is not just that big companies like superstores seem to be able to get their own way, sometimes by something near to corruption, against a large part of local opinion – there were always some, those with cars, who supported them – but the kind of country we would like to live in is never discussed. Tony Blair promised that it would be different under New Labour – we would all be involved, as stakeholders. It was a lie. The Private Finance Initiative contracts provide for no consultation. They lay down the law for 25 to 35 years, sometimes more. We are just not asked for our opinions. Community Health Councils, which had some rights of consultation over PFI, are now to be abolished.

The heart of the matter is the kind of country we want to live in. Is it really a country of towns and housing estates without shops or space for recreation, huge out-of-town superstores and private sports centres, long journeys to work by car on overcrowded roads through congested and polluted streets to a vast factory, warehouse or open plan office, to work at speeds and pressures about which we were not consulted and had not the opportunity to challenge? Alright, in answer, we must agree that some lucky ones will be able to work at home on their personal computers, and get away to Benidorm or Mallorca for a couple of weeks in the sunshine, but what space will there be around our homes for children to play, for gardening and recreation? If we leave it all to the private sector initiatives, none of these matters will come into the calculation of profit and loss.

Space and fresh air have become the two most sought after wants of most people after they have met their immediate needs of food and water, clothing, shelter, and security. Yet, they are in desperately short supply. This is not because, densely populated though we are in many parts of the British Isles, there is not enough land. Urbanisation still only covers about half the land and the demands of agriculture are declining. It is because our town and country planning is at fault. A million new houses have to be built in the next decade to meet the housing needs of smaller families and the present homeless. If this is met by privately built and financed houses, the largest number will be crowded onto the smallest area and no provision will be made for space to allow for parks and gardens or for easy access to work places and shops. It is a staggering challenge, but there can be no doubt that the space, fresh air and ease of access to work and shops will only be possible if public provision within a plan based upon the widest consultation is made central to the solution.

One particular aspect of the Private Finance Initiative and of privatisation and the closure of manufacturing in general has been the reduced role of the trade unions. Several of the new businesses involved in PFI have been reported to have refused to recognise trade unions for collective bargaining: examples are WT Foods, which was founded by a major Labour donor (£100,000 in 1999), and WS Atkins, the engineering and construction firm. Noon Products, of which Gulam K.Noon, a major Labour donor (£100,000 in 1999), has been reported to have refused recognition of the GMB Union at the plant in Southall, although 90% joined up. Even some of the old businesses like Shell have been criticised by the TUC for delinquency. The British Retail Consortium, the supermarkets lobbying organisation make the claim in relation to the minimum wage legislation, that they were 'influential in persuading the government and the Low Pay Commission' to hold the level down to £3.60 per hour and introduce a separate lower rate, not just for young people, but for returners to the labour market.' Union pressures were evidently not so influential.

We saw earlier the persistent efforts of Lord Simon on behalf of the Government to water down or even to block measures being introduced into European Union directives to provide for workers' rights in the case of takeovers and mergers and in the laws on competition. While workers' organisations can often appeal to the conventions agreed under the auspices of the International Labour Organisation, ensuring that they are complied with depends on strong organised action on the ground. Many of New Labour's newly introduced laws concerned with conspiracy, sympathetic strike action, the rights of assembly and demonstration and the protection of property make this kind of organisation much more difficult.

Town and Country Planning

It is not only workers' rights that are being ridden over rough-shod by the privatisation and Private Finance Initiatives of New Labour. We have seen that communities and even local councils have been side-stepped by the developers of superstores, new hospitals and housing estates. But there is something much more involved in the transport of goods and travel to work. The placing of supermarkets out of town is always designed to make use of the motorway system, so as to avoid congestion in the towns. Warehouses are also located close to the motorways. In both cases the railways which were built to go into the town centres are cut out of the picture. The result of declining rail traffic has been declining profits and reduced services and a vicious circle of decline. The recent rail disasters were the result of cost saving on maintenance. It is the same with new factories, new offices and new housing. These are being established increasingly near to the motorways. The result is that motorway traffic itself is becoming congested and seriously polluted, as anyone will know, who is unfortunate enough to have to use the M25. Worse even than this, less and less work is available near to the old town and city settlements and public transport in and around the towns ceases to be readily available. In many parts of the country now it is absolutely necessary to have a car in order to go to work. Not only is a large part of the weekly wage absorbed by travel costs, but stress and tension mount and some people cannot afford a car and face a very limited range of local jobs. So inequalities grow.

All this is the direct result of the breakdown of what had been established as ground rules for town and country planning and of then giving power to private capital to seek the most profitable options. George Monbiot offers a terrifying list of examples in a chapter which he heads: 'How to Buy Planning Permission: The Department of the Environment's Conflicts of Interest'. The conflicts arise, he argues, because a department combining environment, transport and the regions has become both a promoter and a regulator of development. It seems that its promotional work has become enlarged at the expense of its regulatory role, and promotion has come to be defined in the words of a departmental report of January 1999, entitled *The Economic Consequences of Planning to the Business Sector*, as the establishment of 'clear pro-active policies ...' to assist 'business development'. The report claimed that business was being hampered by 'an increasing anti-development mood.' A Department consultation paper entitled *Modernising Planning: a Progress Report* of April 1999 announced the 'speed up' of the planning process in response to 'business need'. The paper suggested that only 'major landowners' and 'local groups with a membership of 50 people or more' should be allowed to speak at public inquiries and dissenters would have to join a membership organisation before they would be heard.

We do not need to look further than some of the names and companies represented among the 'fat cats' on the Task Forces cited in earlier chapters to understand what is happening in modernised planning. Apart from them there are the lobbying groups, most especially those of the Freight Transport Association, the House Builders Federation, the Construction Industry Council and

Construction Federation, who must all have been delighted to read in the 1998 Annual Report of the Department of the Environment, Transport and the Regions that Mr. Nick Raynsford, the Housing Minister, would be working to 'improve the effectiveness of trade associations and other groups.' Those groups and organisations like Green Peace, Friends of the Earth and the Council for the Protection of Rural England, whose aim is the protection of the environment including the green belts, are up against powerful forces.

Lord Sainsbury presides over 16 Foresight Panels in the Office of Science and Technology, which like the Task Forces we looked at earlier, seem largely to be controlled by businessmen rather than scientists and without representatives on them of trade unions, environmental groups or other voluntary bodies. Some indication of the thinking of these Panels can be derived from comments of The Retail and Consumer Services Foresight Panel, chaired by Sir John Banham, the head of Tarmac. In a report published by the Department of Trade and Industry in January 2000, entitled *Progress through Partnership, 15 – Retail & Distribution*, this Foresight Panel warns of the 'potentially dire' impact of growing concerns about the environment, which must lead to 'increasing difficulty in carrying out green field development coupled with attempts to restrict traffic and reduce congestion ...'

With such foresight, we should be forewarned and forearmed. What is being proposed for public and private partnership is nothing less than the privatisation of public space – whether it be with megastores, shopping precincts, branded villages, city malls, sports centres, hypermarkets, or theme parks.

Chapter Seven
A Way Out of the Dilemmas?

The argument of this booklet does not end with the fall from grace of Peter Mandelson. It is not concerned with Mandy's madness, Blunkett's blunderings or Cook's cookery. It is about a project widely regarded as 'Blair's project' to construct a whole new social formation around the cooperation of New Labour with British Business. Conspiracy theory might point the finger at one or two conspirators on either side of the new alliance. The fact is that it was convenient for both parties (small 'p') to come together at this time. The Labour Party had lost its mass base in organised industrial labour to technological change; British capital had lost its strength in industrial production to new producers overseas. The two moved towards each other by a sort of mutual osmosis without clear pre-determination. The result is not only a new economy but a new politics. The ground where they have met and become entwined is the public services of the country. The result has been to take out of political discussion a great part of the national infrastructure – health, education, social protection, transport and the location of housing and industry – and to place it all in the arbitrament of the market.

What has been happening in Britain, and to a lesser extent elsewhere in the more advanced industrial countries, is the ending, perhaps not yet final, of the progress over more than a century of a political movement built up to protect ordinary people from the worst excesses of the exercise of power by private capital over their working conditions and daily lives. Through municipal socialism and socialist measures at a national level power was slowly but surely chipped away from the owners of capital to do what they would with their money. Much more success was achieved by Labour in the reduction of income inequality than in tackling the unequal exercise of power; and even income inequalities have been growing again. Some challenges to the power of capital in the workplace had for a time been rewarded. Failing rail services, mining and steel making were nationalised together with the public utilities of electricity, gas, water and telephones. The public road system was extended and maintained. Some bastions of popular power were created. Of these the greatest was the National Health Service with free treatment on demand, although medicines, dentistry and spectacles have been made subject to payments. Second to the NHS a comprehensive free education system was established and slowly extended up the age groups. Some degree of social security was ensured for all in sickness, unemployment and old age. Land was not taken out of the hands of a small number of very large private owners, but the planning permission of local government authorities was required for changes in its use. Housing was for a time a major responsibility of local councils.

The result of these measures introduced by government legislation was a mixed economy of private and public enterprise. Often the public share was made subordinate to the private, for example, through keeping coal prices down and through other forms of milking the nationalised industries. The public share in the mix was any way much reduced by Mrs Thatcher's government, as private capital sought to built up its holdings in the more advanced industries of gas, electricity and tele-communications. Mining, steel making and the railways were closed up or allowed to run down to make way for alternative new investment. What New Labour has done is to open the way for private capital in the rapidly expanding education, health and information services, while manufacturing is increasingly taken over by foreign investors. This is the story we have seen unfolding here. But we have shown strong reasons for questioning not only the social justice of the result but equally the economic efficiency and sustainability.

Alternative Ways Forward

It would not be desirable simply to return to the old models of the nationalised industries or even of the pre-market-managed NHS. They were all built on principles of large scale operation and centralised bureaucratic planning that were hardly open to worker participation or consumer accountability and would in many cases now be unsuited to modern technology. There is real advantage to-day in reducing the scale of operations especially if this enables those most closely involved as workers and consumers to understand what is being done, so as to participate in day to day decisions and to contribute to long-term planning. There will still, however, have to be some central control over the allocation of resources between different needs if anarchy is not to result and the most vociferous claimants are to be reconciled to the overall judgement of the whole nation when presented with alternative plans.

There is no doubt that there will have to be some form of taking back into public control of certain privatised industries and services if the needs of the public are to be met; and this may involve strong central control at national and even international level. The most obvious example is Railtrack, where public opinion is demanding this, but there is an equal case for the water companies and the energy industry as a whole and telecommunications to be put on a new publicly controlled basis which recognises the close linkages already existing throughout Europe. The use of regulators has simply failed.

The several privatisations that are now proposed by New Labour – including the London Underground and Air Traffic Control – must be halted. There is overwhelming public support for this, revealed most clearly in the election as London's mayor of Ken Livingstone, who fought against all the odds largely on this issue. What has to be ensured in all re-nationalisation proposals is that the interests both of the workers and of consumers are formally represented. How this is to be done must be the subject of another publication.

The real disaster to be tackled is the £16 billion or £20 billion (or is it more?) of Public Finance Initiative contracts already signed in Health, Education, Housing, Prisons, Roads. We have established here the case for stopping any new ones. It is not enough to propose as a second best, very much second best, that all new contracts should include clauses requiring the repayment of windfall or excess profits. The whole business of PFI must be stopped, just as Labour spokesmen, many of them now in government, insisted when they were in opposition.

It will be said that stopping the existing contracts would involve huge compensation payments, which may appear to be an insurmountable objection. They should simply not be paid. A reasonable settlement would have to be reached, which ensured that taxpayers cease at a certain date to continue the payments contracted for. If this is not done, in the not so long run the cost of the payments incurred by the NHS for building new hospitals and by local authorities for new schools will begin to stretch the tax system beyond bearing. The result will be closures and the NHS might be able to buy back bankrupt activities for a song, but the distress and discontent in the process would be great.

In the short run, if contracts are broken, there might be some immediate confusion, which existing contractors would make much of, but a new basis for financing health and education could be established under firm public control. It would still be necessary in the case even of public sector provision to strengthen the various forms of inspection, regulation and accounting, in particular to require the publication of details in contracts with construction companies, which are now withheld as being 'commercially sensitive'. One valuable form of accountability consists in the reports of the House of Commons Public Accounts Committee. Unfortunately, these appear months and even years after the events under investigation, by which time there is not much to be done except by admirable muck-rakers like Paul Foot. It would be a considerable advance for the House to give the Public Accounts Committee much more resources so as to be able to complete reports more expeditiously, and we will discuss this further.

Remedying Inequalities

Any economic system based on the drive for private capital accumulation is going to generate inequalities and the greater the freedom for capital, the greater will be the inequalities. If there are real difficulties in restraining capital, which we will consider later, then at least taxation can be employed to redistribute income. We have seen that the results of tax changes under New Labour had actually been to increase inequality in post tax incomes. The argument that the rich must be bribed and the poor penalised to make the economy work has been rubbished by the group of Cambridge economists whom we quoted earlier. Higher rates of taxation of the rich would overcome many of the objections that are raised against universal non-means tested benefits and pensions, since this extra income would be subject to tax. Excess profits taxes were a device adopted during the Second World War to deal with company profits made as a result of monopoly positions granted to companies under government contracts. The same argument could be used against PFI profits where the so-called risk factor is the ground for higher than normal profits, but where in effect the Government guarantees the security of the contract and is prepared, as in the London University Hospital contract, to provide for any over-run in costs.

It is always the case that unequal distribution of income really reflects unequal distribution of power. The real shift in the social formation which we have been looking at is a shift of power. Representatives of the very largest accumulations of capital in Britain have been invited into the seats of power in a way that has gone far beyond the practice of Conservative Governments except in time of war. It is quite clear from what we have seen that the Task Forces, Panels and Foresight Groups, consisting mainly of businessmen without trade union or non-governmental organisation representation, are not just advisory bodies, but have real decision-making power. This has been made possible by the extraordinary concentration of power under New Labour in the hands of the Prime Minister and, to a somewhat less extent, the Chancellor of the Exchequer. This is in part the result of New Labour's overwhelming majority in the House of Commons, in part the result of the deliberate dismantling of the traditional representative organisation of the Labour Party and the Trade Unions.

The extent of this centralisation of power can be illustrated not only by the creation of 320 Task Forces with 2500 members all appointed and none elected, but also by the proliferation of appointed Special Advisers in the office of the Prime Minister and in each of the main Government Departments. There are now 78 special advisers with 29 in the Prime Minister's Office alone, for which the total salary bill is reported to be £10.8 million. The influence of these advisers is not only that they provide the spin for all Government policies but that they provide a necessary coordination of a centrally determined policy to prevent it being side-tracked by opposing groups – not of course Her Majesty's Opposition which has no idea how to oppose what is an extension of traditional Conservative policy

– but by trade unions, environmentalists and other dissident non-governmental organisations.

What should be done with the Task Forces is to dismantle the lot. If some advisory bodies of experts are needed in addition to the civil service, then Parliament should insist that the trade unions, non-governmental organisations and non-business experts should be equally represented along with the businessmen. The alternative to appointed Task Forces is a great strengthening of the House of Commons committees. Here there arises a further dilemma which any honest man or woman who has ever sat in a Parliament has immediately come to recognise. It is literally just a 'parlement', a talking shop, and cannot really act, despite its legislative powers, and this is for one reason. Advancement not only to government office but equally to serving on Committees of the House depends on the patronage of the Prime Minister. Unless you are an independent – and people with a personal reputation such as that of Martin Bell are likely to be few and rarely interested in such politicking – you will only be elected in the first place and certainly only re-elected, if you are a Party member and toe the Party line, and that is today in effect the Party leader's line. As more and more of the general public recognise the sleaze which follows inevitably from personal patronage, MPs will learn to act more independently as representatives of their constituents.

To reduce the powers of the Prime Minister, however, something more than independently minded MPs will be needed. New Labour has talked much about the need for constitutional change, but the only change that matters is that the Prime Minister must be shorn of the rights which he or she has of acting through decision by the Crown and Privy Council without consulting Parliament. The Privy Council consists of any Lords or cabinet ministers or ex-cabinet ministers whom the Queen and Prime Minister agree to call together on any occasion. It was under this remaining royal prerogative of the Privy Council and not by the will of Parliament that the decisions were made to go to war in the Falklands, in the Gulf and again in Yugoslavia. Parliament was subsequently asked to debate and confirm these decisions, but by then it was a bit late. It is not only wars that are decided in this way but many Government decisions and appointments, of Task Forces for example, are made by 'Orders in Council' and only debated in the House thereafter. All this residue of a feudal order must be ended if the power of the people is to be a reality.

The European Dimension

There are of course other dilemmas. A major difficulty in the way of any action either to tax the rich or to restrict the activities of Big Business is that they will take themselves and their money and businesses elsewhere, to places which will treat them better. This argument can be exaggerated. The UK remains a valuable market and for many a nice place to live in. Shifting funds to offshore trusts in such tax havens as the Channel Islands, the Isle of Man or the Bahamas already takes place on a vast scale – many thousands of billions of pounds – which Gordon Brown once promised to investigate and tax. The promise has not been fulfilled, but it could be, however embarrassing for certain members of the Government. We have seen examples of some 'blind trusts' where big businessmen, who have become ministers like Lord Sainsbury and Lord Simon or Geoffrey Robinson, have deposited their wealth, in order to avoid the accusation of conflicting interests. One such trust managed on the owner's behalf but without his intervention amounted in the case of Lord Sainsbury to £1400 million.

To prevent businesses, which one would wish to keep in the UK, and to prevent managers and investors from abandoning the UK for easier locations, it would be necessary to achieve some international agreements about the harmonisation of taxation and the regulation of competition over wage rates and workers' rights. The danger is of a downward movement such as Mr Blair has encouraged, to become 'the most business-friendly country' in Europe. A start could indeed be made in the European Union, where much of the movement of capital takes place. Mr. Oscar Lafontaine as German Finance Minister was called 'the most dangerous man in Europe' and soon lost his job for proposing measures of harmonisation, which would have stopped the downward drift in levels of company taxation. We saw earlier at least two occasions when Lord Simon acted on behalf of the Government to block or water down European Commission directives on workers' rights. Labour members of the European Parliament, far from supporting these rights against such manoeuvring, were in the front of demands that 'our' business interests should not be restricted by requiring consultation. Arlene McCarthy, for the British Labour group of MEPs, went so far as to say in discussion in the European Parliament of a draft directive, that an amendment introduced in the Parliament went against 'our primary objective ... to protect our investors ... against hostile action or poison pills.' Lack of consultation in the case of the Corus closures left the Government powerless when the company acted to sack 7,000 workers.

The advantage for Britain of a European connection is that most European countries enjoy public services and working conditions that are far superior to those in the UK. On almost every count of provision for health, for education, for social security and old age the UK comes at or near the bottom of the 'league table' of European countries. The details were shown in a study called *Defending the Welfare State*, published by Spokesman in 1998 with support from a wide range of experts on the subject. Nothing has happened to improve the standing of Britain's welfare services since that date which would make it necessary to change the conclusions. Indeed, in some respects, and especially in the prevalence of poverty and increasing inequalities, things have got worse. The Cambridge economists to whom we referred earlier made a special point which was quoted of the superior economic efficiency as well as greater degree of social justice in European countries which had followed other policies than those of New Labour.

We can hope in time to call such people as Arlene McCarthy to order, though the electoral process for the European Parliament at present makes that very difficult. The beginnings of an opposition to New Labour from the left are barely visible, but the introduction of proportional representation and the establishment of European-wide parties would reveal new forces and alliances. What we have concluded about the unsustainable nature of Government policies suggests that discontent will grow. At the present moment the mood of the public seems to be cynical rather than openly critical. There are many things the public dislikes – poor schools, dirty hospitals, broken rails, mis-sold pensions, congested roads, polluted towns, street crime, uncontrolled floods, and, perhaps above all, sleaze in high places. The Mandelson story leaves a very nasty taste behind it, and his personal resignation is not likely to be the end of that story. The one thing the Tory Opposition can be relied upon to do is to expose New Labour sleaze. It is a case of the pot calling the kettle black, but it can become cumulatively damaging. All this is negative criticism and lacks a positive message. We cannot expect to see a political change until there is a clear alternative for people to embrace.

When an alternative is presented to the corruption and injustice of the story we have told here it will have to comprise a realistic picture of the kind of country we should all want to live in. All forms of health care and child care and the care of the disabled and handicapped would be free. Education would be free at every age right through to life-long learning. Housing would be available at reasonable rents with access by foot to shops and parks and gardens and to many work places. There would be a wide range of opportunities for work in production and services with appropriate training built in. There would be no discrimination at work on grounds of gender, race, age or sexual orientation. Conditions and hours of work would not be unnecessarily long, dangerous or exhausting. Pensions for the aged and invalid and payments during sickness and unemployment would be provided on a universal scheme based on contributions related to income. Planning of land use, road and rail transport, industrial location and the balance of urban and rural activities would be subject to the most open examination and discussion. In all walks of life, at work and at home, in all workplaces and public institutions management would be subject to agreed forms of consumers' and workers' controls.

We have the resources for all this. We just have to find how to change the system from one of private greed to that of public gain.

Sources

British Medical Journal, BMA House, Tavistock Square, London, WC1H 9JP

Cambridge Journal of Economics, Oxford University Press, Great Clarendon Street, Oxford, OX2 6DP

Capital and Class, 25 Horsell Road, London, N5 1XL

Department of Trade & Industry, http://www.dti.gov.uk

The Ecologist, PO Box 326, Kent, ME9 8FA

Environment Agency, http://www.environmentagency.gov.uk/files/shame

Ethical Consumer, Unit 21, 41 Old Birley Street, Manchester, M15 5RF or at www.ethicalconsumer.org

Naomi Klein, *No Logo*, Flamingo, Harper Collins, 77-85 Fulham Palace Road, London, W6 8JB

The Labour Research Department, *Fact Service*, 78 Blackfriars Road, London SE11 8HF

London Review of Books, lrb.co.uk

George Monbiot, *The Captive State: The Corporate Takeover of Britain*, Macmillan

Public Audit Select Committee, House of Commons, http://www.parliament.uk/commons.selcom

Red Star Research, http:/www.red-star-research.org.uk

The Treasury, http://www.treasury.gov.uk

UNISON, http:/www.unison.org

Who's Who, 2000, www.whoswho.com

* * *

Also available from Socialist Renewal

Welfare Reform
Means-tested versus Universal Benefits
By John Grieve Smith
(pamphlet no.1 £2 ISBN 0 85124 643 5)